# SHE WHO DARES

*An Eight-Week Study on Learning to Live Dangerously for God*

## KRISTI HUSEBY

*To my dear sweet mama, who was the first to show me
what daring to live dangerously for God looked like.
A strong, yet gentle woman who boldly embraced the path God asked her to walk,
from the frozen tundra of Alaska to the heat of California,
and the humidity of Georgia. Faithful to the end. Even as her body took her down,
her tenacity to follow Jesus with her whole heart remained unshakeable.*

# CONTENTS

# INTRODUCTION

PRAYING A DANGEROUS PRAYER WAS NEVER EVER ON MY BUCKET LIST. Never even a blip on my radar. I have always run in the opposite direction of anything risky, "dangerous," or out of my comfort zone. But God has done an amazing work in this ordinary girl and this is His story.

My parents were missionaries in the frozen tundra of Alaska, and on a thirty-degrees-below-zero day in the little town of Glen Allen, I entered this world. Surprisingly, growing up in Alaska was a lot like living in a fairy tale, where fear was absent and "happily ever after" reigned (at least it felt like that to me). There was sledding down snow-covered hills. Ice-skating on the lake out our front door. Roaming the woods with my friends. Popping wild blueberries into my mouth and feeling the juice run down my chin. Watching the myriad colors in the dancing Northern Lights. Hiding behind cabbages grown to astounding size from the midnight sun. Laying on my back gazing up at the immense starry sky. I loved Alaska. It was where I belonged.

*But* when I was eight years old, my parents moved our family from Alaska to CALIFORNIA and my fairy tale world vanished.

I was abruptly thrust into a world filled with fear. Everything was completely foreign. Instead of roaming the woods to my heart's content, I now played in a fenced-in backyard in hundred-degree weather. I could no longer see the starry sky because of the light pollution, and snow was only a distant memory. Our doors stayed locked all day and I was warned *never* to open it to anyone I didn't know. Most nights my pillow was wet with tears, and fear became my constant companion.

# THE COMPANIONSHIP OF FEAR

Fear lurked around every corner. Waited for me in every room. Stalked me in the dark. Whispered to me as I walked home from school. Counseled me in every situation. Shouted to me in my relationships and burrowed its way deep into my heart. I would lay awake most nights; imagination running wild, diligently listening for any unusual creaks in the house.

One night, out of sheer exhaustion, I had fallen asleep only to awaken to the sound of someone fiddling with the lock on our front door. Terror shot through my body like a bolt of electricity. I laid there, heart pounding, unable to move. I was sure the thing I had dreaded most—someone breaking into our house and murdering us all in our beds—had just become my reality!

With a sudden spurt of adrenaline, I bolted out of bed and sprinted into my parents' room, shouting, "There's someone coming in the front door!"

I saw my mom jump out of bed to reach for me. Her mouth was moving, but I couldn't understand what she was saying. Fear overwhelmed me and I stood there shaking from head to toe. I heard *someone* step into the room and I whirled around, expecting to see our axe-wielding murderer. Instead, I saw my dad, and I crumpled into a ball on the floor.

I hated this fear. I hated what it was doing to me. I hated how much control it had over me. I begged and pleaded with God to take it away. I would recite Psalm 56.3 over and over. "What time I am afraid, I will trust in Thee." (Can you tell that I learned it in the King James Version?) But no matter what I did, I just couldn't shake this fear that had invaded my life and stolen my peace. I felt completely out of control, living at the mercy of fear. So I did what Scarlett O'Hara did in the movie, *Gone with the Wind*, when she stood in the barren field, shook her fist at God, and swore she would never be hungry again. I shook my fist at God and resolved to take as much control as I possibly could, convinced I could do a better job than He had done.

It was an insidious deception that entwined itself around my heart and weaved its way into my life. Staying in control at all cost, became a way of living for me. Life became a cover-up, so no one would see the terrified, imperfect, shame-driven me.

# KINGDOM OF ME

By the time I was a young adult, my "relationship" with God was a checklist. If I looked good on the outside and did all the right things—didn't disappoint my parents, didn't sleep around, didn't do drugs, said the right words, and went to church every time the doors were open—God would love me more. But I struggled reading my Bible and spending time with Him. Deep down, I knew my heart was terribly broken. Secretly I believed my heart was like the irreparable Humpty-Dumpty: "All the king's horses and all the king's men couldn't put Kristi together again."

So, I did the best I could to fix myself by continuing to check the list and be the good girl.

*No* became my word of choice. "No, I can't; I'll look like a fool. No, I won't; that's too risky. No, that is not in my comfort zone.

No, I can't trust You, God; You don't feel safe and quite frankly, it's a whole lot easier to trust me than it is You."

If you had asked me if I was a follower of Jesus, I would have wholeheartedly said yes! Technically, I was. I had invited Christ into my life at a young age. But honestly, I was following me, not Jesus. I was in the process of building my own little kingdom and working hard to have God fit into it.

I knew I wasn't perfect, but secretly I thought God had gotten a good deal when He got me. I couldn't see how fear had knitted itself into every area of my life. How needing to be in control was keeping God at arm's length. How my striving for perfectionism was holding me back from being honest with myself and God. I thought *this* was following.

# FROM RELIGION TO RELATIONSHIP

I have learned God loves us where we are at, yet He pushes us to be more. More of who He wants us to be. Sometimes it's a gentle nudge, but sometimes it feels like He's pushing us off a cliff. At other times, He allows us to continue down our destructive paths until the consequences catch up to us, then He moves in to do His work in our lives.

Allowing my fears to run rampant in my life held me back repeatedly from experiencing the freedom Jesus brings. But God wanted more, not from me but for me. **God didn't see me as a hopeless cause but rather as a daughter, whom He longed to have return home.**

Through a series of heartaches; a broken and unreconcilable relationship with a close friend, a marriage in trouble, and a wayward son, God began to dig deep into my life to root out the deceptive lies and beliefs. And I finally let Him bring His light down into the dungeon of my soul. It wasn't pretty. This refining process has been anything but pleasant. Each new movement of God in my life has felt like surgery without anesthetic.

- When my husband said, "I give up! It doesn't matter what I do, I won't ever please you." God exposed the ugliness of my own sin in our marriage, and God refused to let me point the finger at my husband and blame him for all our problems.

- When God used a coworker to call out the pride hidden in my heart. I was angry and wanted to lash back, "Don't you see how prideful you are?" God in His quiet conviction revealed the truth in what she said and, once again, brought His light into the darkness of my soul.

- When God challenged me to call a stranger back and confess that I had lied to her to get what I wanted. God used this to open my eyes to who I was actually trusting—ME.

It's never enjoyable to see our brokenness and sin in all its ugliness. But when we allow God to shine His light into the dark places of our heart, to do His refining work, this is where true delirious freedom is found.

In each of these instances, God was stripping away the ugly, forging within me a tender heart, and giving me the "want to" to let go and follow Him. To surrender fully to His way and His work in my life. With each new step of surrender, He was teaching me to trust, and in the trusting, I discovered fear no longer had power over me. I was finally free to pray a dangerous prayer: **"God I want your way not my way."**

God used this prayer and the heart change that came with it to radically shift the course of my life.

**Refusing to give power to our fear enables us to dare to live dangerously for God**.

Friend (because you're reading this book, I consider you a friend), I so want you to experience this transforming freedom and power only God can give when we say, yes to His way. That's why I wrote this book.

I'm convinced, we will always have something to be afraid of—it's the nature of living in this broken world. **The real question is, will we allow our fear to be bigger than our God, or will God be bigger than our fear?**

I'm still in the process of learning to let God be bigger than my fear. For me, I believe it will be a forever earthly battle. The latest struggle has been in writing this book. Even now, I'm breaking out in a cold sweat. I feel stupid, inadequate, and small. "You're not enough. You'll never be enough." This is the dialogue that runs in my head. And the temptation to listen and believe is strong.

Recently, I read Mark Batterson's book, *Primal: A Quest for the Lost Soul of Christianity*. He posed this question: "Do you have any God ideas that are being held ransom by reasonableness?"[1] It grabbed me and would not let go. Reasonableness. What?

Here's what I wrote in my journal after reading this:

*At the core of why I haven't followed through on this God idea of writing a book is fear! I've cloaked my fear with good excuses, like . . . I don't have time. I don't know where to begin, or what to do first. I don't have clarity. I'm too distracted. It just isn't reasonable for an ordinary girl like me to write a book . . . But peel all the excuses away and at the heart is fear—Can I really write a whole book? Will someone even read it? Will it be cohesive? Am I too old?*

That day, I realized . . . once again, I have given fear power in my life and allowed it to keep me barricaded in my comfort zone. Safe, comfortable, and mediocre.

**This is what our enemy—whether it is Satan or our own desires—is good at: paralyzing, rationalizing and demanding reasonableness.** Fear tethers us and keeps us from never stepping out in radical faith. Never fully following. Never completely letting go.

Jesus said, "The thief comes only to steal and kill and destroy. I came that **they may have life** and **have it abundantly**," (John 10.10 ESV).

The thief has come to steal . . . Our peace. Our joy. Our purpose. Our courage. Our hope. Our life. Our identity. Fear has been his tool of choice. And we have succumbed to his tactics.

---

1 Mark Batterson, *Primal: A Quest for the Lost Soul of Christianity* (Colorado Springs: Multnomah, 2009), 130.

For far too long we, who are daughters of the King, have let:

OUR FEAR PARALYZE US.

*our busyness distract us.*

OUR STRONGHOLDS CONTROL US.

*our view of God distort us.*

OUR MEDIOCRITY DIMINISH US.

*our comfort pacify us.*

OUR SHAME CRIPPLE US.

Take a few minutes to reflect on this list.
What obstacles resonate the most? Circle one or more.

# NOW IS THE TIME

Now is the time to unleash the power of God's Holy Spirit living in us. Now is the time to be the daughters of the King He created us to be. Now is the time to leave the past behind and rise up. Now is the time to say no to fear and yes to God!

This is a journey we take together. So, let's get to it! I can't wait to see what God does with an army of His princess warriors who are committed to saying yes and daring to live dangerously for Him.

# HOW TO USE THIS BOOK

This book is designed to assist you in exploring God's Word not for knowledge but for transformation; to realign your focus and see your life through His lens. **So often there is a gap between what we know and declare, and how we live.** The tendency will be to read this book for the knowledge we can obtain. It's so much easier to pursue knowledge than real heart transformation. For some of you, much of the truth in this book will not be new to you, but **the real question is are you living the truth, you know**? Reading for transformation instead of knowledge allows God's Word to change us from the inside out. It invites Him to tread down the stairs of our own private dungeons and shine His light on the ugly hiding in our hearts.

Each chapter will have five lessons. It is designed for you to process through each chapter bit by bit, rather than biting off the whole. This gives God the space to speak to you through His truth and implant it in your heart. As you read, you'll notice that I've highlighted parts of Scripture passages throughout to help emphasize different words and phrases.

## Day 1: An Ancient Story

We will examine the life of a woman from the Bible. Each narrative is written so you might see the women as real people, not just stories in an old book. Then you will have the opportunity to do your own "treasure hunt" as you take a deeper look into the Scripture; see the story for yourself and discover the truth that lies within it.

My hope is that we will see these ancient women in a new light; as real, ordinary people who were imperfect, afraid, but trusted in an extraordinary God and ultimately dared to say yes! May we be inspired and encouraged by their acts of faith to do the same.

# Day 2: God's Bigger Story

Here we will look at other passages of truth scattered throughout the Bible as we explore the theme of the chapter. From stories of victory, failings, and struggles from others, we will discover how God has worked to implant His truth in their hearts and transformed their lives.

# Day 3: Dig Deeper into the Story

Through guided questions, you can delve deeper into your own study of God's Word.

These simple questions are designed to encourage you in your own discovery of the truth. My hope is that you will grasp how you can study God's Word for yourself. Do not discount the simplicity of the questions. Learning how to ask simple, yet profound, questions enables us to take our own exploratory journey of God's Word.

Self-discovery of truth through the illumination of the Holy Spirit is where true transformation happens. Think about it . . . how much more is something implanted in your heart when you discover it for yourself, rather than having someone else tell you about it?

As you read the Scripture, have a pen handy and circle, star, underline, and make boxes around the observations you see. Here are some things to look for as you read the Scripture:

- Key words
- Advice, admonitions, warnings, and promises
- Contrasts, comparisons, illustrations
- Repetition, progression of ideas

Ask who, what, where, why, how questions as you read. (One of my favorite questions to ask is "What could they have done instead?" Thinking about other options that our character could have done often brings deeper understanding to what they actually did.)

The Scripture is printed in each chapter to enable you to have an interactive experience with the passage.

I encourage you to forego a commentary or a Bible with study notes, (until after you have done your own study, and met with your small group to discuss) so that you can experience your own self-discovery. It is okay to sit with a portion of Scripture you don't understand or questions you cannot answer.

# Day 4: Pause and Reflect on the Story

Did you know there are thirty-one references to *meditation* in the Bible and only three mentions of the word *study*? And yet, what has been our go-to method with God's Word? *Study* is an important element in understanding the Scriptures God has given us, but it should never take the place of "being" with God in His Word.

Think about it this way. What if your husband came to you and said, "I have this book of questions and I want to study you." Then he proceeds to ask you questions and write them in his little book. After you've answered all of his questions, he closes the book and says, "Great, now I know all about you." What would your response be?

Would it go something like this? "Hey, wait a minute. Just because I answered a few questions about myself doesn't mean you know me. Put the book down and let's have a conversation." Sure, he might learn some things *about* me, but that doesn't mean he truly *knows* me.

God gave us His Word so we can know Him. But too often our time alone with God looks more like us filling out superficial answers in a workbook than sitting with God and His Word, reflecting and listening to who He says He is. Uniting our hearts with His. This is where real relationship happens.

The focus of this fourth lesson is to spend time with God in His Word; reflecting, meditating, and journaling on the truth from it, while asking the critical question, "How will I let God's truth transform my life?"

This reflective space is designed for you to be with God in His Word. It is not a time for study. It is a place for you to let God's Word sink into your soul and experience Him through His Word. This is what the Bible encourages when it says to meditate on God's Word. Don't rush through it. Take time to be with God.

# Day 5: Dare to Live the Story

In this section, we will look at a contemporary counterpart to our ancient woman of the Bible. These are modern-day women, who are imperfect just like our ancient women, but are still saying yes to God and daring to live dangerously. My hope is that you will see it is possible, not just in Bible times but now, to say YES! to God and dare to live dangerously for the Kingdom.

# GUIDELINES

What we think on becomes what we believe. What we believe dictates how we act. If we focus on implementing a self-help program to have better behavior, then eventually we will fail because our beliefs and our thinking have not changed. For true transformation to happen, we must allow God to dig down deep and uproot the patterns and habits of our thinking, which will then change what we believe and ultimately how we will act.

1. This book is designed for you to spend five days each week, so you can process the truth bit by bit rather than biting off the whole. I believe we give God more opportunities to speak and move in our hearts when we take our time and not try to cram everything in all at once. But the choice is up to you.

2. This book is not about discovering the perfect formula for achieving your goals. You won't find a list of things you can check off to improve yourself. God desires us to go deeper. He wants to get at the root of our sin problems. But I must warn you, this is not the easy path. It is uncomfortable and hard, but it is the only way to true transformation.

The Apostle Paul says it this way, "Don't copy the behavior and customs of this world, but **let God transform you** into a new person **by changing the way you think**," (Romans 12.2). It is impossible to truly transform ourselves, but the problem comes when we think we can.

This book is about allowing God to journey with us down into the dungeons of our soul where fear, lies, and deceptions hide. It's about giving Him permission to carry them out into His glorious light and set us free from the burden of self-betterment.

It is a whole lot easier to implement a self-help program, following easy steps to "health," than it is to let God uproot the false beliefs and wrong thinking in our lives. But this uprooting is where true change happens.

So if you find yourself in the middle of this book, saying, "Kristi, would you just tell me what I need to do to change?" I understand. It was how I felt when I was struggling with letting go of my pride.

I had done a spiritual examination of my life and had asked some key people in my life to answer some questions regarding my spiritual condition. A co-worker identified that I was prideful. I was furious when I found out she felt this way about me, and I wanted to rip her a good one. How dare she! I could tell her a thing or two about herself. But I felt God stop me in my tracks and gently challenge me to examine if what she said was true or not. It didn't take long for me to realize that even though I had been "working on my pride", I was still prideful in my heart. I might not have been speaking pridefully, but it was coming out in my attitudes and facial expressions. I was rattled, if I was still prideful after working so hard on it, how was I going to rid myself of this pride? I knew it wasn't going to be through reading another book. This was something God was going to have to root out of my life.

God wants to do a great work in you. He is not calling you down the easy of path of self-betterment but the difficult way of letting Him transform you by changing the way you think. Will you let Him? I dare you!

*Week 1*

# DARE TO BUILD A YES-LIFE

*"God wants it all. And it's in the exchange of what we want for what God wants that we experience the adventure and freedom and power of saying yes to God."*

—Lysa TerKeurst[2]

Dearest Lord, as we venture into this journey of daring to live dangerously, guide us to Your truth. Open our hearts and teach us not to settle for anything less. We want to experience the adventure, the freedom, and the power of saying yes to You. Because this is where true life is found. It's in Jesus's name, we pray. Amen.

---

2 Lysa Terkeurst, *What Happens When Women Say Yes to God* (Eugene, OR: Harvest House Publishers, 2018), 78.

# DAY 1
## AN ANCIENT STORY
### Rebekah

It was a normal day. There was no quickening of her heart, no stirring in her soul to indicate that this day would be anything but the same as yesterday.

Laying on her bed mat, Rebekah raised her hands above her head and gave her body a good stretch. She could smell the fragrance of a meal being prepared, and her stomach rumbled as she made herself ready for the day. It was life as usual—a meal, chores, and a walk with her friends down to the spring to get water.

She didn't see him at first. The stranger sitting by the well.

*Where did he come from*, she wondered? *I've never seen him here before. Why is he here? His accent is strange.* So many thoughts flooded her mind, but she held them inside. With the water jar on her shoulder, she lowered her head and walked past him.

She could feel his eyes on her as she dipped the jar into the spring. Then he spoke to her.

"Will you give me a drink?"

After giving him some water, she asked, "Would you like me to give your camels water as well?"

He was startled by her question but said nothing and simply nodded his head. Again, she sensed him watching her as she continued to fill up her jar of water over and over as she gave his camels a drink. She wasn't afraid. She could see he was a man of peace.

*But what is he doing here?*

When she finished, he reached into his satchel and took out a nose ring and two beautiful gold bracelets and placed them in her hands.

"What is your name and whose daughter are you?" he asked.

"I'm Rebekah, the daughter of Bethuel. My grandparents are Nahor and Milcah."

"Would they have a place for my men and me to stay the night?"

"Yes, we have plenty of straw and feed for your camels and guest rooms for you and your men."

Later that evening while eavesdropping on her parent's conversation at dinner with the stranger, Rebekah learned the reason he had come to her village.

He was from her Uncle Abraham! He was seeking a wife for Abraham's son, Isaac.

Rebekah had heard stories of her Uncle Abraham; how he had packed up his belongings, said goodbye to his relatives and left the only home he had ever known. They had often wondered what had become of him. Wondered if he was still alive? Where he had settled? How many children they had?

Rebekah was deeply moved by hearing this simple man's story. Animatedly he described the long journey and the experiences he had along the way. He shared with them how he had prayed to the God of his master Abraham, before he had left, that God would direct him to the home of his master's relatives. When he arrived in the village, he explained to them how he had prayed for God to bring the chosen woman to the well. He shared how before he had even finished praying Rebekah was there! But he hadn't just prayed for the right woman to come to the well, he had also prayed that this woman would offer to give his camels a drink, so that he would know she was the right one for Isaac.

Rebekah listened in wonder and amazement at this stranger's story. And suddenly it dawned on her—*I am the one he prayed for*. It was staggering to think about and yet, God had directed this man so specifically to her. She could not deny it.

As a young girl, she had often dreamed of the man she might someday marry. But never in her wildest imagination did she foresee this happening.

She listened with trepidation as she heard her parents offer her hand in marriage to Isaac. This was a man she had never met or even heard about until today!

That night Rebekah laid awake wondering what her new life would be like. It felt like she was standing on the edge of a cliff.

Saying yes meant leaving the only home she had ever known and stepping into the unknown. *How can I say goodbye forever to my family and my friends? Who is this Isaac person? Is he kind and gentle or rough and cruel? Where will I live? How can I give myself completely to someone I've never even met?*

In the quiet of the night, she knew there were no answers, just a simple request, "Will you trust Me?"

The next morning, the servant man was anxious to begin the long journey home. This wasn't what her parents had planned. They wanted time to give her a proper goodbye, but they agreed that if Rebekah was willing, they would let her go.

"Are you willing to go with this man?" her parents asked.

Rebekah knew in that moment what her answer would be. She was jumping off the cliff. She was stepping into the unknown. Her faith journey had begun.

Without a moment's hesitation and without reservation, she replied, "Yes, I'm willing to go."[3]

---

3 Note from author: Each of these ancient stories are written so you can see the people as real women with real struggles, just like you and me. Remember, these stories are based on Scripture combined with the author's imagination of what it might have been like.

# Taking a Deeper Look

*In this section, it is your turn to take a deeper look at this story in God's Word and see for yourself the truth that lies within. There is space on the right side for you to make your own notes and observations as you read. After reading the Scripture and making your own notes and observations, there are questions to serve as a guide as you search for the treasure within the story. If you don't know the answers to some of the questions, it's okay. Not knowing all the answers is not a bad thing. My hope is that it will cause you to think more deeply and explore Scripture in ways you might never have, if just given the answer.*

## GENESIS 24.36–57

[36] *"When Sarah, my master's wife, was very old, she gave birth to my master's son, and my master has given him everything he owns.* [37] *And my master made me take an oath. He said, 'Do not allow my son to marry one of these local Canaanite women.* [38] *Go instead to my father's house, to my relatives, and find a wife there for my son.'*

[39] *"But I said to my master, 'What if I can't find a young woman who is willing to go back with me?'* [40] *He responded, 'The Lord, in whose presence I have lived, will send his angel with you and will make your mission successful. Yes, you must find a wife for my son from among my relatives, from my father's family.* [41] *Then you will have fulfilled your obligation. But if you go to my relatives and they refuse to let her go with you, you will be free from my oath.'*

[42] *"So today when I came to the spring, I prayed this prayer: 'O Lord, God of my master, Abraham, please give me success on this mission.* [43] *See, I am standing here beside this spring. This*

## NOTES & OBSERVATIONS

Refer to page 8 for guidance on how to dig deeper into the story.

*What could be some of Rebekah's fears?*

*is my request. When a young woman comes to draw water, I will say to her, "Please give me a little drink of water from your jug." *<sup>44</sup>*If she says, "Yes, have a drink, and I will draw water for your camels, too," let her be the one you have selected to be the wife of my master's son.'*

*<sup>45</sup>"Before I had finished praying in my heart, I saw Rebekah coming out with her water jug on her shoulder. She went down to the spring and drew water. So I said to her, 'Please give me a drink.' *<sup>46</sup>*She quickly lowered her jug from her shoulder and said, 'Yes, have a drink, and I will water your camels, too!' So I drank, and then she watered the camels.*

*<sup>47</sup>"Then I asked, 'Whose daughter are you?' She replied, 'I am the daughter of Bethuel, and my grandparents are Nahor and Milcah.' So I put the ring on her nose, and the bracelets on her wrists.*

*<sup>48</sup>"Then I bowed low and worshiped the Lord. I praised the Lord, the God of my master, Abraham, because he had led me straight to my master's niece to be his son's wife. *<sup>49</sup>*So tell me— will you or won't you show unfailing love and faithfulness to my master? Please tell me yes or no, and then I'll know what to do next."*

*<sup>50</sup>Then Laban and Bethuel replied, "The Lord has obviously brought you here, so there is nothing we can say. *<sup>51</sup>*Here is Rebekah; take her and go. Yes, let her be the wife of your master's son, as the Lord has directed."*

*<sup>52</sup>When Abraham's servant heard their answer, he bowed down to the ground and worshiped the Lord. *<sup>53</sup>*Then he brought out silver and*

*gold jewelry and clothing and presented them to Rebekah. He also gave expensive presents to her brother and mother.* <sup>54</sup>*Then they ate their meal, and the servant and the men with him stayed there overnight.*

*But early the next morning, Abraham's servant said, "Send me back to my master."*

<sup>55</sup>*"But we want Rebekah to stay with us at least ten days," her brother and mother said. "Then she can go."*

<sup>56</sup>*But he said, "Don't delay me. The Lord has made my mission successful; now send me back so I can return to my master."*

<sup>57</sup>*"Well," they said, "we'll call Rebekah and ask her what she thinks."* <sup>58</sup>*So they called Rebekah. "Are you willing to go with this man?" they asked her.*

*And she replied, "Yes, I will go."*

(FURTHER READING: GENESIS 24.1–67)

# REFLECTION

1.  How would you describe the faith of Abraham's servant? In what ways did he **demonstrate** his faith in God?

2.  How did Rebekah demonstrate her faith in God?

3.  Don't discount the fears Rebekah faced because her life was so different than yours. What fears in your life might be holding you captive?

4.  What is your takeaway from the story of Rebekah?

John Ortberg, in his book *Faith & Doubt*,[4] says, "The best indicator of my true beliefs and my purposes are my *actions*. They flow out of my mental map about the way things really are. What I say I believe might be bogus. What I think I believe might be fickle. But I never violate my idea of the way things are. I always live in a way that reflects my mental map. I live at the mercy of my ideas about the way things really are. Always. And so do you."

Understanding this is crucial for spiritual growth and transformation."

If we are to change, we must take a hard look at what our true beliefs are. We must examine what our actions are displaying and ask the hard question, "If I'm living this way, what is my core belief about God?" Only then can we begin to allow God's Holy Spirit to infiltrate our lives and change the mental map of our hearts.

---

4 John Ortberg, *Faith and Doubt* (Grand Rapids: Zondervan, 2008), 48

# DAY 2
# GOD'S BIGGER STORY

*With every request from God, we have just two responses.*
*One response gives life, the other takes it.*
*One empowers, the other cripples.*

## The Debilitation of No

When I was a teenager, I came home one day with a reckless plan to give all my money to a missionary family in our church. I was so excited and passionate about this idea and couldn't wait to tell my mom what I planned to do.

While growing up in my parent's household, I was taught how to manage money. Their method of choice was the standard envelope system. There were envelopes for saving, giving, and spending. All my life, my parents have been in full-time Christian ministry, which meant we didn't have much money. So the little we had was frugally used.

My mom was careful, cautious, and never extravagant—she couldn't afford to be. She would spend hours each week, clipping coupons and scouring the grocery store ads for sales. She was a master at getting the most bang for her buck.

I dashed in the door that day, excitement bubbling over in me. "Mom, guess what? I've decided to give all my money to our missionary friends! Isn't that great?"

I was sure she would be overwhelmed by my generous spirit and was shocked when she didn't respond with a resounding affirmation to my master plan. Instead, her response shook me to my core, and I allowed an ugliness to take shape in my spirit which would have lasting effects for years to come.

"Do you think that is wise?" she asked. "How are you going to pay for necessities? You can't just recklessly give all your money away, you need to think carefully about this. You have money set aside for giving, why don't you use that?" (All good questions to ask, I might add, so please don't be too hard on my mom—she was dealing with an impulsive and reckless teenager who was continually coming home with hairbrained ideas.)

Looking back—because it's true that hindsight is 20/20—I now know that this was a perfect opportunity for her to ask the kinds of questions that would help me explore whether this was just my own big idea or a prompting of the Holy Spirit to sacrificially give. It was an opportunity to say, "Let's pray about this together and if you still feel led to give, then by all means do it."

My mom's response to my grandiose idea was like sticking a pin in a balloon. Deflated, I chose to give nothing. Not even the money I had set aside for giving. But the deeper fall-out from this experience was what I allowed to happen in my heart. Generosity wasn't even a word in my vocabulary. I chose to let this simple no create a lifetime of stinginess in my heart.

I can't help but wonder what would've happened if she had said yes to my crazy reckless idea. Would I have had a more generous spirit? Would I struggle, even to

this day, with sacrificial giving? I recognize it was my choice to react the way I did. I didn't have to let her questions discourage me and keep me from giving. But I did. And ultimately, it led me down the path of saying no to God.

*What happens in your heart when you say no to God?*

*How has your rebellion affected your relationship with God?*

Is there ever a time when we should say no to God?

Saying no to God disables, debilitates, and holds us captive to our fear.

## Just Say Yes

But, what happens when we say yes? What potential is unleashed in us? When Rebekah said yes to God, He changed the course of her life, and this choice ultimately gave

her the privilege of being a part of God's redemption plan for His people.

Because I was in the habit of saying no to God, my life was a miserable mess. I was stingy and controlled by fear over our financial circumstances.

God used a simple spiritual assessment questionnaire, to point out the stinginess I was harboring in my heart. It opened my eyes to how much of this systemic tightfistedness stemmed from the habit I had built long ago. It was time for a change, time to tear down the wall.

This battle was all too familiar, I felt like God and I had been working on this stingy stronghold for most of my life, and there was a part of me that just didn't want to have to face this issue yet again. But God continued to press into my heart and call me to change.

So I prayed, "God I'm willing to give, just give me an opportunity and I'll take it." It didn't take long.

One busy afternoon, I was standing in line at the grocery store and there was a woman in front of me who was trying to use her food card the government provides for those in need. Every time she put in her password a notice would say her card wasn't recognized. She was getting more and more frustrated by the minute and finally told the cashier that she would need to set her groceries aside and call her caseworker. My heart went out to her—how embarrassing this must be.

And then I heard a small quiet voice[5] say, "Kristi, why don't you pay for her groceries?"

**What?** *Well, you know Lord if it were just twenty dollars . . . but its more than double that! That is just way too much to give to a stranger.*

"Why don't you pay for her groceries?" the voice was a little louder this time.

*What will my husband say if I spend that much money?*

"Why don't you pay for her groceries?" I couldn't get the thought out of my head.

The battle raged within my heart, as the cashier rang up my bill. Shaking inside, I contemplated . . . *Should I do this? I don't know—yes you do! Quit fighting, isn't this what you prayed for? Okay, okay. I give in. I got it. I'll do it.*

I turned to the cashier and casually asked, "Would it be okay if I paid for her groceries?"

The cashier was a little taken aback, "You know it's fifty dollars?"

"Yes, I know and I'm fine with that. Would it be alright?" Like it was no big deal. Ha! (If she only knew what had transpired in my heart.)

---

5 Note from the author: How does God speak to us? He does speak in an audible voice but more often than not, it is a prompting in our heart from the Holy Spirit. How do we discern if this is God's "voice/prompting" in our lives? Here are some important questions to ask: 1) Does it align with Scripture? This is the most important question to ask. Contradiction of Scripture is a red flag that this prompting or voice is not from God. 2) Is this something I would naturally do? (like give money to a stranger). If it aligns with Scripture and it is not something we would naturally do, then it is up to us to trust this is the movement of God in our hearts and obey. 3) What do other godly people say regarding this? It's easy to go to people who we know will tell us what we want to hear but we need to seek those that will tell us the truth even if it hurts.

The transaction took just a moment, then she looked at me and asked, "Do you want to tell her?"

I knew what the Lord wanted me to do. I said, "No, I think you should tell her."

And I walked out of the store—no, actually I floated!

I couldn't believe what I felt; this incredible joy filled my soul as I walked out in wonder and amazement that God would give me such an incredible gift! What were the odds that I would be behind this woman at just the right time to help her? I could see God's hand all over this ordinary visit to the market.

So why do I quibble over a few measly dollars when my Heavenly Father has given me a gift that all the money in the world could not purchase?

## Building a Yes-Life

In saying yes there is life, there is joy, there is power. I wish I could say this stingy heart was set free that day but, unfortunately, I can't. I was so excited about what had transpired and what God had done in my heart, I told God, I was willing to do it again if He would just give me another opportunity.

A few weeks later, I was out with my son having lunch at a restaurant in town. As I was paying the bill and leaving a tip, I felt prompted to leave the twenty-dollar bill I had in my wallet, which is a rarity. But instead of doing it, again I argued. *She doesn't deserve a twenty-dollar tip. Our meal wasn't even twenty dollars.* And I left with the twenty-dollar bill in my wallet.

As I got into my car, I was immediately assaulted with regret. I knew I should've said yes, but again I let the stinginess rise up in my heart and dictate my response. I sat there in the car that day and cried. How could I have let this happen again when just weeks earlier I had experienced such freedom. I told the Lord how sorry I was and if He would just give me another opportunity, I wouldn't argue, I wouldn't question, I would just do.

It was *over a year* before I felt the prompting of the Lord in my heart to give outside the norm. This time, I responded with a resounding yes. No questions. No arguing. Just plain obedience. And oh, the freedom from this simple obedient act. It was indescribable.

Responding with our first yes brings freedom, whereas a no wraps the chains of fear around us and holds the Holy Spirit hostage.

Saying no to God meant the Israelites had to wander around in the wilderness for forty years! Saying no to God caused Jonah to be thrown overboard and swallowed by a big fish. Saying no to God, kept the rich young ruler from following Jesus. Saying no meant that he missed knowing Jesus, seeing Him turn water into wine, raising people from the dead, and spending an eternity with Him.

But saying yes to God gave Shadrach, Meshach, and Abednego the courage to say no to the king and the opportunity to be a part of an incredible miracle. Saying yes to God made Abraham the father of many and ultimately the earthly forefather of our Savior. Saying yes to God gave Elijah the power to raise a young boy from the dead and defeat the enemies of God. Saying yes to God allowed Paul to travel worlds away sharing the Good News of Jesus.

Saying yes changes everything! Saying yes declares our obedience and aligns our hearts with God's which in turn gives us the faith to surrender everything. Saying yes opens wide the doors of our hearts.

**Saying yes to God, isn't just words we say, but a life we live.** It's training our hearts to say yes. It's cultivating a yes-life and letting the roots run deep.

A yes-life brings freedom, and the result is courage even in the face of scary as the Holy Spirit unleashes His power in our lives and we are forever changed!

# DAY 3
# DIG DEEPER INTO THE STORY

## MATTHEW 7.24-27

*"Anyone who **listens to my teaching and follows it is wise**, like a person who builds a house on solid rock. Though the rain comes in torrents and the floodwaters rise and the winds beat against that house, it won't collapse because it is built on bedrock. But anyone who hears my teaching and doesn't obey it is foolish, like a person who builds a house on sand. When the rains and floods come and the winds beat against that house, it will collapse with a mighty crash."*

## NOTES & OBSERVATIONS

Refer to page 8 for guidance on how to dig deeper into the story.

*What's the difference between listen and hear?*

1.  What characteristics define the person who builds a strong foundation (the rock) and the one who builds their life on the sand?

| ROCK CHARACTERISTICS | SAND CHARACTERISTICS |
|---|---|
|  |  |

In this passage of scripture, what does the person who builds their life on the rock and the person who builds their life on the sand have in common?


How are they different?



2.  Why is it important to build a strong foundation?



3.  What foundation best describes you and why? Before you answer, think back to our conversation with John Ortberg, remember "we live out our true beliefs".



4.  How do we, as followers of Jesus, build our life on the ROCK, so that when the storms come and the waters rise, we will stand strong? (What did Rebekah do?) How is this a yes-life?

5. What choices or changes do you need to make today to begin to build a strong foundation on the Rock?

*For who is God except the LORD? Who but our God is a solid rock?*
*God is my strong fortress, and he makes my way perfect.*
*He makes me as surefooted as a deer, enabling me to stand on mountain heights.*
*He trains my hands for battle; he strengthens my arm to draw a bronze bow.*
*You have given me your shield of victory; your help has made me great.*
*You have made a wide path for my feet to keep them from slipping.*
—2 SAMUEL 22.32–37

*\*This is a place for you to journal your thoughts and/or prayer.*

# DAY 4
# PAUSE AND REFLECT ON THE STORY

*This section will encourage you to spend time with God in relationship with Him. This is not a time for you to rehash what knowledge you have gained but to allow God to examine your heart . . . to sit before Him and listen.*

> *Investigate my life, O God, find out everything about me;*
> *cross-examine and test me;*
> *Get a clear picture of what I'm about;*
> *See for yourself whether I've done anything wrong—*
> *then guide me on the road to eternal life.*
>
> —Psalm 139.23–24 (MSG)

How has God spoken to you regarding what you have just read and studied in this first chapter?

What challenged you?

What encouraged you?

# Contemplative Prayer

**Read aloud, listen to the words, and be still for 1–2 minutes:**

> Jesus said to his disciples, "If any of you wants to be my follower, you must give up your own way, take up your cross, and follow me. If you try to hang on to your life, you will lose it. But if you give up your life for my sake, you will save it. And what do you benefit if you gain the whole world but lose your own soul? Is anything worth more than your soul?"
>
> —Matthew 16.24–26

**Write down 1–2 simple observations:**

**Read aloud again and reflect for another 1–2 minutes:**

> Jesus said to his disciples, "If any of you wants to be my follower, you must give up your own way, take up your cross and follow me. If you try to hang on to your life, you will lose it. But if you give up your life for my sake, you will save it. And what do you benefit if you gain the whole world but lose your own soul? Is anything worth more than your soul?"
>
> —Matthew 16.24–26

**What in this passage touches my life today?**

**Read aloud again and respond for another 1–2 minutes:**

> *Jesus said to his disciples, "If any of you wants to be my follower, you must give up your own way, take up your cross and follow me. If you try to hang on to your life, you will lose it. But if you give up your life for my sake, you will save it. And what do you benefit if you gain the whole world but lose your own soul? Is anything worth more than your soul?"*
> —MATTHEW 16.24–26

**What is God inviting me to do today?**

**Read aloud again and rest for another 1–2 minutes:**

> *Jesus said to his disciples, "If any of you wants to be my follower, you must give up your own way, take up your cross and follow me. If you try to hang on to your life, you will lose it. But if you give up your life for my sake, you will save it. And what do you benefit if you gain the whole world but lose your own soul? Is anything worth more than your soul?"*
> —MATTHEW 16.24–26

**Ask nothing, simply rest in the presence of the Lord.**

*Write down what God has spoken to you through His Word.*

# Cultivating a Yes-Life

We see the potential a yes-life unlocks, but how exactly do we nurture, develop, and maintain a yes-life? In the following chapters, we will dig deep into Scripture and explore what it looks like to cultivate this kind of life. We'll sit at the feet of Jesus and learn from Him.

Is it possible to dare to live a yes-life? Where our first response is yes instead of no? Where we live a life in tune with God—ready to go, do, say, and be whatever He desires? Where fear no longer has the last word in every discussion? Where we continually lean into Him and listen to His voice instead of the myriad of voices around us? Is it possible? I believe it is!

**Would God ask us to dare to live this life if it was not possible?**

Let's start saying yes today!

*Write out a prayer of commitment to God. Don't be afraid to share your hesitations and your struggles, then invite Him to do His good work in you.*

# DAY 5
## DARE TO LIVE THE STORY
### *Kay*

She was only eight years old when it began.

Every Tuesday evening, she would lumber up the stairs to stand on a scale and be judged by her father. She always failed.

Kay's father was obsessed by appearances. He expected everything and everybody to make him look good, including his eight-year-old daughter. He was a narcissist in the purest sense of the word. He amassed great sums of money and then would lose it in some crazy scheme or another. He became a millionaire many times over. Kay was eighteen years old, when her father walked out and started a new family with a woman just two years older than she.

The hurt accumulated over a lifetime of interactions with her father left Kay bruised and broken. But God saw this shattered and hurting girl. He saw the sleepless nights when her pillow was drenched with tears, and He loved her.

One day Kay decided to open her heart to God, and she was never the same again. She had a new Father now, a Father who loved her just the way she was. A Father whose love had no conditions, no demands, and no expectations.

But her old life colored her perspective of God. Her perception of her heavenly Father was twisted by her earthly father's behavior. Her spiritual foundation was built on half-truths, suppositions, and rules; so when the "Tsunami" hit, pieces of her foundation and the little faith she had were swept away in the torrent of flood waters. Even though she had been a follower of Jesus for many years, the strong foundation she thought she had was no longer to be found.

"I'm sorry to tell you this but we have arrested a young man who was sexually molesting young children in the nursery of your church, and we believe your son was one of those who was abused."

*What! How could this happen?* It was more than her mind could grasp. Rage welled up inside of her, and God was the recipient of the full force of her anger. *How could You allow something like this to happen to my son! How could You let me worship You without giving me any inclination or warning that this was happening to him?*

Feeling betrayed and broken, Kay put her Bible on a shelf and walked away from God. But crazy enough, God refused to walk away from her. She would go for long walks trying to get away from His presence. She would raise her fist in the air and cuss and swear and say horrible things to God demanding He leave her. But He didn't. This is how she described it, "It wasn't a condemning or judgmental presence, He was just there."

Through His quiet, gentle presence, God began to melt the ice around her heart. Then one day, about a year later, she glimpsed her Bible on the shelf, and something moved in her spirit. She picked it up, blew the dust off and opened it. As she perused this long-forgotten book, she noticed something . . . all the verses she had underlined were hard things about God—His anger, justice, wrath. Verses like those in Job 9.12–13: *If he snatches someone in death, who can stop him? Who dares to ask, "What are you doing?" And God does not restrain his anger. Even the monsters of the sea are crushed beneath his feet.*

Through the prompting of the Holy Spirit (even though she didn't realize it at the time), Kay wondered what her friend, Jill, had underlined in her Bible. She picked up the phone and called her. "Jill, what do you have underlined in your Bible?"

Jill read from Lamentations 3.22–24: "*The faithful love of the LORD never ends! His mercies never cease. Great is his faithfulness; his mercies begin afresh each morning. I say to myself, 'The LORD is my inheritance; therefore, I will hope in him!'"*

It was as if Kay was hearing God's Word for the very first time. She wondered how she could have missed those verses. Kay told her friend, "I think I need a new Bible. Would you be willing to walk with me through God's Word and help me to take a fresh, new look at who God says He is?"

As Kay journeyed through God's Word that year with her friend, she began to form a true picture of who God is. She began to know Him. Instead of squishing Him into the box she wanted Him to fit in, instead of picking and choosing which truths she wanted to believe, she let God define who He is. She opened the doors of her heart to God, and she, like Job, was finally able to say, "I'd heard about you, but now I've seen you." As she allowed her roots to run deep into God, He built an unshakeable foundation within her.

Kay didn't know it at the time, but this was just the beginning. God was preparing her for one of His biggest asks ever.

It had been years since she'd seen her father, and frankly, she was good with that. But while on a trip to Florida, she felt prompted to go and see how he was doing. The thought of it made her sick to her stomach, but she knew she had to. Trembling inside, she stood on his doorstep and hesitantly knocked. She didn't recognize the man who answered the door. It looked like he had just climbed out of bed and it was the middle of the day; hair mussed up, dirty white T-shirt, and wrinkled shorts. His place was a mess. There was rotten food in the fridge, a loaded gun under his pillow, and he was talking crazy out of his mind. It was all she could do to not run screaming from the place.

The visit shook her to the core. On the long drive home to Michigan, she heard the ask: "Will you bring your father home to live near you and take care of him?" It took her breath away. *How can I even contemplate something like this? Just the thought of it makes me want to curl up in the fetal position. How will I ever be able to cope with being near him, much less care for him?*

As she rumbled with God and her own emotions, she knew deep down she had to say yes. With a surety that came from truly knowing her Savior, she chose to obey. God would be with her, He would give her the strength and the fortitude to live out this audacious calling on her life.

Kay moved her Dad into a nursing home near her house. The first five months he was there, the man was toxic. She wanted to throw herself out of the car, every time he would ride with her. But she continued caring for him and as the months marched on a miracle happened. He began to soften—the harsh demeanor waned, the toxic words vanished, and he became a sweet old man. And God began to heal her wounded heart as she walked in obedience.

Two years later, as her dad lay close to death, Kay stood by his bedside holding his hand, singing the old hymns. And while she sang, she realized for the very first time . . . she loved him![6]

# What About Us?

Kay could've said no. In the eyes of the world, this was a crazy, unthinkable ask. Her dad didn't deserve her care. He had dumped her long ago. She owed him nothing.

But what would've happened if Kay had said no to God? Would she have experienced the healing she needed? Would the regret haunt her? Would she be stuck in unforgiveness, unable to grow?

Even though it didn't make sense even to her, she obeyed and, in that simple obedience, unleashed the flood gates of blessing on her life. She has no regrets.

---

6 Story used by permission.

Kay experienced the power of God's Holy Spirit—the power that raised Jesus from the dead—in her life. As she surrendered her will to His, He filled her heart with a supernatural love for a father who didn't deserve it. God set her free, her faith grew strong, and she found healing from a lifetime of abuse and shame.

This is the simple, whole-hearted obedience God asks of all His followers: ***Dare to live dangerously and Just. Say. Yes.***

**Note from Author:** God doesn't call all of us to do what Kay did. Maybe there is a relationship in your life where it would be dangerous for you to remove the boundaries you have had to put in place to keep you safe. God knows your situation. He sees the hurt and the pain. You can trust His heart and dare to live dangerously through your obedience in whatever He calls you to do.

## My Prayer For You

*Now to the God of peace—who brought up from the dead our Lord Jesus, the great Shepherd of the sheep, and ratified an eternal covenant with his blood—may You equip _____ with all she needs for doing Your will. May You*
          *(insert your name)*
*produce in her, through the power of Jesus Christ, every good thing that is pleasing to You. All glory to You, God, forever and ever! Amen.*

(Prayer based on Hebrews 13.20–21)

## Will you dare to live dangerously and build a yes-life?

*Week 2*

# DARE TO KNOW YOUR GOD

*"One of the most wonderful things about knowing God is that there's always so much more to know, so much more to discover. Just when we least expect it, He intrudes into our neat and tidy notions about who He is and how He works."*

—JONI EARECKSON TADA[7]

Jesus, you bridged the gap our sin created between us and you. And now we have the privilege of an intimate relationship with the God of the universe. But we are so easily distracted with accumulating facts about You instead of knowing You intimately. We are so easily satisfied with letting others tell us about You instead of spending sacred time with You alone. Teach us to see You, know You, experience You. Reveal Yourself to us through Your Word. Show us how to love You with all our heart, with all our soul, with all our mind, and with all our strength. Amen.

---

7 Joni Eareckson Tada, *Glorious Intruder: God's Presence in Life's Chaos* (Colorado Springs, CO: Multnomah Books, 1989), 94.

# DAY 1
# AN ANCIENT STORY

## *Mary*

MARY HAD JUST FINISHED WASHING THE clothes in the stream near their house. The basket was heavy in her arms and she was glad to be able to set it down. She could hear the birds singing in the trees nearby as she began to hang up the clothes to dry in the heat of the sun.

A shadow fell across her basket as she reached to pick up another wet piece of clothing. Startled, she looked up and her heart jumped in her chest. She hadn't heard his footsteps. Where had he come from? Who was this man?

He was like no one she had ever seen, and his words confused her. "Greetings to you, favored one. The Lord is with you!"

It was fear like she'd never known before. Frozen, she struggled to breathe and to hear what this man was saying.

But then this giant of a man replied with words so tender: "Don't be afraid, Mary, for you have found favor with God! You will conceive and give birth to a son, and you will name Him Jesus. He will be very great and will be called the Son of the Most High. The Lord God will give Him the throne of His ancestor David. And He will reign over Israel forever; His Kingdom will never end!"

She felt the fear loosen its powerful grip and finally was able to speak. "How is this possible? I'm not married, and I've never even slept with a man."

The words she heard next boggled her mind and sent a million questions racing around in her head.

"The Holy Spirit will come upon you, and the power of the Most High will overshadow you. So the baby to be born will be holy, and he will be called the Son of God. What's more, your relative Elizabeth has become pregnant in her old age! People used to say she was barren, but she has conceived a son and is now in her sixth month. The word of God will never fail."

The questions dissipated, and the last threads of fear melted away as she listened to this unusual being.

Mary bowed her head in reverence and surrender to this man, who she finally understood was not of this world.

"I am the Lord's servant," Mary said with confidence. "May everything you have said about me come true."

And then he was gone.

Dazed and shaken, Mary's legs began to wobble, and she collapsed onto a nearby rock.

*What just happened?*

*Did I really have a conversation with a supernatural being or could this have been some figment of my imagination? Could I have drunk too much wine at dinner last night?*

*What was it he said?* She forced herself to remember everything, replaying this strange conversation over and over in her mind.

And it was then she remembered something he'd said. It had to do with her Aunt Elizabeth . . . He had said she was pregnant, but wasn't she a hundred years old?

As she sat there on the rock, she remembered how Aunt Elizabeth and Uncle Zechariah had prayed for so long for God to allow Elizabeth to get pregnant. But it had been years since she had heard anything. It was obvious they had given up hope a long time ago.

Why had they not told her family? If she was in her sixth month, it would be obvious to everyone.

She jumped up, clapped her hands together and exclaimed, "I've got to go and see them, then I will know for sure if this is real or just something I imagined." Adrenaline coursed through her body as she raced into the house, laundry completely forgotten.

It took her a couple of days to make all the arrangements, but soon she had her bags packed. Laden with gifts from her family for Zechariah and Elizabeth, she began the journey.

*Why is this donkey so slow!* She just couldn't seem to get there fast enough. She was so anxious to see them both.

Dusty and dirty from the hurried trip, she arrived on their doorstep and began to question her rash decision to visit them. *What will they think? What if it isn't true?* Questions filled her mind as she raised her hand and hesitantly knocked.

A moment later Aunt Elizabeth was there, standing in the doorway. She watched as her aunt's questioning countenance transformed into pure joy when she realized who it was.

Awe filled Mary's heart, as she gazed upon her sweet Aunt Elizabeth. Mary hardly recognized her. She seemed to be glowing. Her soft face was a map of wrinkles, and her big beautiful baby bump was there for all the world to see. *An old woman pregnant? Such a contradiction of sight.*

All the doubts and questions she'd hashed and rehashed on the journey, fell away as her dear Aunt Elizabeth pulled her into the sweetest embrace Mary had ever known. Somehow, in some miraculous way, she knew Mary's secret.

"God has blessed you above all women, and your child is blessed. Why am I so honored that the mother of my Lord would visit me? This baby growing inside me jumped when I heard your voice. You are blessed because you believe God will do what He said."

And in that moment, Mary knew it wasn't just something she'd conjured up in her imagination, it wasn't a dream, it was true . . . this promise from the angel was really happening. Mary's heart and lips poured out praise to her God.

# *Taking a Deeper Look*

*In this section, it is your turn to take a deeper look at this story in God's Word and see for yourself the truth that lies within. These questions are intended to be a guide as you search for the treasure. If you don't know the answers to some of the questions, it's okay. Not knowing all the answers is not a bad thing. My hope is that it will cause you to think more deeply and explore Scripture in ways you might never have, if just given the answer.*

## LUKE 1.26-56

[26] In the sixth month of Elizabeth's pregnancy, God sent the angel Gabriel to Nazareth, a village in Galilee, [27] to a virgin named Mary. She was engaged to be married to a man named Joseph, a descendant of King David. [28] Gabriel appeared to her and said, "Greetings, favored woman! The Lord is with you!"

[29] Confused and disturbed, Mary tried to think what the angel could mean. [30] "Don't be afraid, Mary," the angel told her, "for you have found favor with God! [31] You will conceive and give birth to a son, and you will name him Jesus. [32] He will be very great and will be called the Son of the Most High. The Lord God will give him the throne of his ancestor David. [33] And he will reign over Israel forever; his Kingdom will never end!"

[34] Mary asked the angel, "But how can this happen? I am a virgin."

[35] The angel replied, "The Holy Spirit will come upon you, and the power of the Most High will overshadow you. So the baby to be born

## NOTES & OBSERVATIONS

Refer to page 8 for guidance on how to dig deeper into the story.

*What do these verses tell us about Mary?*

*How does Mary feel when the angel makes his appearance?*

will be holy, and he will be called the Son of God. ³⁶What's more, your relative Elizabeth has become pregnant in her old age! People used to say she was barren, but she has conceived a son and is now in her sixth month. ³⁷For the word of God will never fail."

³⁸Mary responded, "I am the Lord's servant. May everything you have said about me come true." And then the angel left her.

## MARY VISITS ELIZABETH

³⁹A few days later Mary hurried to the hill country of Judea, to the town ⁴⁰where Zechariah lived. She entered the house and greeted Elizabeth. ⁴¹At the sound of Mary's greeting, Elizabeth's child leaped within her, and Elizabeth was filled with the Holy Spirit.

⁴²Elizabeth gave a glad cry and exclaimed to Mary, "God has blessed you above all women, and your child is blessed. ⁴³Why am I so honored, that the mother of my Lord should visit me? ⁴⁴When I heard your greeting, the baby in my womb jumped for joy. ⁴⁵You are blessed because you believed that the Lord would do what he said."

## THE MAGNIFICAT: MARY'S SONG OF PRAISE

⁴⁶Mary responded,

"Oh, how my soul praises the Lord. ⁴⁷How my spirit rejoices in God my Savior! ⁴⁸For he took notice of his lowly servant girl, and from now on all generations will call me blessed. ⁴⁹For the Mighty One is holy, and he has done great things for me. ⁵⁰He shows mercy from generation to generation

*Bible Study Hint: Whenever the Bible gives us specific details, it's important to pay attention to them. The Bible can often cover years in just one sentence, then turn around and give specifics about the color of curtains. Whenever I see these details, I pay attention and ask myself what the author might want us to know or understand through these details.*

*to all who fear him. 51His mighty arm has done tremendous things! He has scattered the proud and haughty ones. 52He has brought down princes from their thrones and exalted the humble. 53He has filled the hungry with good things and sent the rich away with empty hands. 54He has helped his servant Israel and remembered to be merciful. 55For he made this promise to our ancestors, to Abraham and his children forever."*

*56Mary stayed with Elizabeth about three months and then went back to her own home.*

# REFLECTION

It has been four hundred years since anyone in Israel has heard a direct message from God, and one of the first messages is to a teenage girl. Remember this as you answer the following question.

1. How did Mary respond?



2. What do we see in Luke 1.46–55 that indicates how well Mary knew her God? (This passage of Scripture is known as "Mary's Magnificat.") It's easy to get lost in its beauty and forget that these words are pouring out of the heart of an uneducated teenage girl. What does that tell you about her? What does she know?



## LUKE 1.6–22

*When Herod was king of Judea, there was a Jewish priest named Zechariah. He was a member of the priestly order of Abijah, and his wife, Elizabeth, was also from the priestly line of Aaron. ⁶Zechariah and Elizabeth were righteous in God's eyes, careful to obey all of the Lord's commandments and regulations. ⁷They had no children because Elizabeth was unable to conceive, and they were both very old.*

*⁸One day Zechariah was serving God in the Temple, for his order was on duty that week. ⁹As was the custom of the priests, he was chosen by lot to enter the sanctuary of the Lord and burn incense. ¹⁰While the incense was being burned, a great crowd stood outside, praying.*

*¹¹While Zechariah was in the sanctuary, an angel of the Lord appeared to him, standing to the right of the incense altar. ¹²Zechariah was shaken and overwhelmed with fear when he saw him. ¹³But the angel said, "Don't be afraid, Zechariah! God has heard your prayer. Your wife, Elizabeth, will give you a son, and you are to name him John. ¹⁴You will have great joy and gladness, and many will rejoice at his birth, ¹⁵for he will be great in the eyes of the Lord. He must never touch wine or other alcoholic drinks. He will be filled with the Holy Spirit, even before his birth. ¹⁶And he will turn many Israelites to the Lord their God. ¹⁷He will be a man with the spirit and power of Elijah. He will prepare the people for the coming of the Lord. He will turn the hearts of the fathers to their children, and he will cause those who are rebellious to accept the wisdom of the godly."*

*18Zechariah said to the angel, "How can I be sure this will happen? I'm an old man now, and my wife is also well along in years."*

*19Then the angel said, "I am Gabriel! I stand in the very presence of God. It was he who sent me to bring you this good news! 20But now, since you didn't believe what I said, you will be silent and unable to speak until the child is born. For my words will certainly be fulfilled at the proper time."*

*21Meanwhile, the people were waiting for Zechariah to come out of the sanctuary, wondering why he was taking so long. 22When he finally did come out, he couldn't speak to them. Then they realized from his gestures and his silence that he must have seen a vision in the sanctuary.*

3. Both Zechariah and Mary ask a question of the angel after he gives them the message from God. What is the question from each of them and how does the angel respond?

(Luke 1.18–20)

**Zechariah:**


*Gabriel:*


(Luke 1.18–20)

**Mary:**


*Gabriel:*


4. How do the questions of Zechariah and Mary differ from one another?


5. Zechariah was a priest and Mary, a simple uneducated teenage girl and yet, who had the deeper faith? Why did this young teenage girl seem to have a greater faith than the priest?

# DAY 2
# GOD'S BIGGER STORY

THERE ARE VAST AMOUNTS OF BOOKS, podcasts, articles, and weekly sermons devoted to helping followers of Jesus learn a lot ABOUT God. And it's not to say they aren't important, but nothing will replace our own personal, intimate time with God through prayer, being in His Word, and being still enough to listen to His quiet whispers.

It's in this space where we develop a relationship with God that leads to more than just knowing about Him but truly KNOWING Him. Where we learn who He says He is, not just what others say about Him. Where we see His truth and begin to understand His heart. It's where our hearts are knit with His and we begin to understand what the Psalmist was saying when he wrote, *"As the deer longs for streams of water, so I long for you, O God. I thirst for God, the living God. When can I go and stand before him?"* (Psalm 42.1–2).

## Religion over Relationship

A good chunk of my life was spent learning a lot about God. I grew up going to church—Sunday morning, Sunday evening and Wednesday night prayer meeting. I learned all the Sunday school songs, memorized verses, and knew the Bible stories backward and forward. I invited Christ into my life at an early age. I knew I was a sinner. And because I didn't want to go to hell, I asked Jesus to come into my life. However, I didn't understand what it meant to have a love-relationship with God. He was just "fire" insurance.

I told people I had a relationship not a religion. And I thought I did. But the hard truth was—it was just another works-driven religion. It was a check list of dos and don'ts and a boatload of head knowledge. And while head knowledge can be a useful thing in the right place, it can never be a substitute for a relationship.

I was more focused on practicing a religion than cultivating a deep relationship with God, and when the storms of life came, my faith crumbled down around me.

I was disillusioned and disappointed with God for not giving me what I thought I needed, and I began to question the validity of following Him. *Could I be "giving my life" to something that isn't even true?* I wondered.

I saw other people who had a deep and intimate relationship with God. They seemed to know Him so personally. I craved to have what they had, but it always felt like it was just beyond my reach.

Then one very ordinary day, everything changed . . .

# *Falling in Love with Jesus*

I had been taking a class on what it meant to follow Jesus with an undivided heart. And for the very first time, I began to comprehend what it might look like for me to have a love relationship with God.

The instructor first encouraged us to think about what it was like when we fell in love with our husband or boyfriend. How we wanted to spend time with him, how every waking moment was spent thinking about him, and how we took every opportunity to be with him. Next she made this shocking statement: "This is the kind of love God wants to have with you!" *What?* I'd never thought about my relationship with God that way . . . ever.

Then she went on to talk about how we replace our love relationship with God with other things—husband, children, job, beauty, food, etc. They take our time, our money, our thoughts, our energy, and our focus. We love these people and things like we should be loving God, and they end up taking everything from us. These loves become our false gods.

I resonated with what she was saying. I knew this was true of me. The love relationship I had been in for so many years was with food. I thought about food all the time. I would wake up in the morning thinking about what I was going to eat that day. I planned to put the kids down for a nap and have "time alone" with my Dove chocolate bar. I had never seen before how my love relationship with food was stealing me away from a love relationship with the One true God. How I had no room for Him because of this obsession. Food took everything from me and never gave me anything in return except extra unwanted pounds and a tormented mind. It put me on the crazy cycle. Never truly satisfied. Always needing more.

Then something ridiculous began to happen. As I was identifying the false gods in my life, I began to recognize a false god in my husband's life. Isn't that the way it is? Instead of looking at the plank in our own eye, we see only the speck in someone else's eye. This is a tactic the enemy loves to use to keep us stuck in our own crazy sin-cycles.

I was angry because he was spending his free time involved with his "false god," fantasy football and neglecting me. I saw it so clearly . . . it was taking his time, his thoughts, and his attention, not to mention *our* money.

And on this very ordinary day, I was out on my back porch, ranting at God about all of this. "I just want my husband to want to be with me. I don't want to have to tell him he should spend time with me. I want him to say, 'Honey, the guys asked me if I wanted to go and watch the game with them, and I realized it's been weeks since we've been out together. I miss you and want to spend time with **you**.'"

With all my heart, I just wanted him to WANT to be with me . . . And that's when I felt God whisper deep in my soul, "Kristi, that's how I want you to love me." *What?*

In that moment, it felt like the scales fell from my eyes and I finally got it! "You want me to *want* to be with You?"

My mind was in a daze . . . of course, who would want a relationship based on obligation and duty? I for one sure didn't.

An authentic relationship is built on love, not a list of requirements and certainly not duty and obligation. All these years, I had been so wrong. I'd tried so hard to do all the right things and be the good girl, when all along God just wanted me to know Him, love Him, and want to be with Him.

I sat there overwhelmed by His amazing love and patience with me. When I opened God's Word that day, it was as if I had a brand-new Bible. Because for the very first time, I saw that these were not just great truths, but they were truths written for me. They were God's love letters to *me*!

I fell head-over-heels in love with my God that day. I knew He loved me, and I wanted to be with Him. I wanted to see who He said He was, not what someone else told me about Him. I wanted to know what made His heart sad and glad. I wanted to hear His whispers. I wanted to have treasured moments with the Lover of my soul.

The cross and what my Savior did for me was cast into a new light. What more could He do to prove His love for me? I had believed and known for many years that Christ died for me, but somehow it never seemed personal. What I couldn't grasp until that moment, was how intimate and personal this sacrifice truly was. Just as God can hear the individual prayers of each person in the whole world all at the same time, Jesus was thinking of me when He died on the cross. He bore the weight of my sins on the tree that day. Oh, what love—what amazing, heart-stopping love.

# Knowing Versus Knowing About

We can know a lot about someone but never truly know them. And if we only ever know ABOUT them, we will never truly love them.

Let me explain this in another way.

I knew a lot about Robin Williams. He was an amazingly talented man. Incredibly funny and spontaneous and a fabulous actor. In one movie he pretended to be a woman and the next he was a Jew in a Polish ghetto. But what I didn't know was that he had a very troubled soul. And eventually he took his own life. I knew about him but I didn't KNOW him.

I didn't know Robin Williams in the same way I know my husband.

I know whether my husband has had a good or bad day, just by the look on his face or the tone of his voice. I know what gives him great joy and what breaks his heart. I know him because I have spent time with him, lived with him, and experienced life with him. **Knowing someone comes from being in relationship.**

This intimate knowing of someone is what is referred to in the Bible when it says, "Adam knew Eve and she conceived." Intimate knowing means there are no barriers, no walls. We are naked and unashamed, stripped bare of all pretenses.

# Relationship Broken

Before the fall, Adam and Eve had an intimate relationship with God. They walked and talked with God in the Garden of Eden. They were naked and unashamed. But when they disobeyed God, their sin created a barrier in their relationship with Him. Suddenly, they were ashamed of their nakedness; not just their physical nakedness but their spiritual, relational, and emotional nakedness as well. Cast out of the garden, they no longer enjoyed the intimate rela- tionship with God. A huge chasm opened between them and God, because God is Holy and He cannot dwell with sin. This severing of the relationship wasn't just for Adam and Eve, it was extended to everyone who would come after them. The Apostle Paul describes it this way, "*You were his enemies, separated from him by your evil thoughts and actions*" *(Colossians 1.21).* There was no longer any way for man to have a relationship with God.

# Relationship Restored

But God stepped in and bridged the gap, our sin created, between us and Him. He sent His Son, Jesus, to this earth, to live a sinless life and to die a painful death on the cross, taking the punishment we deserved. When Jesus died on the cross, He smashed the barrier for all time and made a way for us to be in an intimate love relationship with God once again.

*Paul continues in Colossians 1.22: "Yet now he has reconciled you to himself through the death of Christ in his physical body. As a result, he has brought you into His own presence, and you are holy and blameless as you stand before him without a single fault."*

And when we acknowledge our sin, believe in Jesus's death that paid the price for our sin, and invite Him into our lives as Lord and Savior, our relationship with God is restored. We are transformed from enemies of God to family—adopted into His family as sons and daughters (see Ephesians 1.5).

We are *holy, unashamed, and blameless as we stand before Him without a single fault!* Notice it doesn't say, "Someday we will" stand holy and blameless before Him without a single fault. God has come to live with us NOW. We are brought into His presence NOW. We can know Him now, all because Jesus made it possible.

To know God and to be known by Him, means we allow Him to kick down our walls and we stand naked before Him; our sins revealed, our deceptions unveiled. The real true us. And the wonder of it all is . . . He still loves us.

# Know → Trust → Obey

There is a difference between knowing about someone and truly knowing them. Do you KNOW your God or do you just know ABOUT Him?

When we know Him, a heart of trust is birthed in us, and trust leads to obedience without question. The measure of our faith is not in how much we know *about* God but in how much we truly trust Him.

A friend of mine told me a story about a couple who was driving across the country. The wife had her nose in a book and wasn't looking at the road, when all of a sudden, her husband yelled, "Lay down!"

And she did. Her unquestioning obedience saved her life that day.

They had come around a curve and were confronted with a jack-knifed semi-truck in the middle of the road. Her husband had just seconds to determine how to save their lives. They smashed head-on into the side of the trailer. If she had not obeyed immediately, she would've been decapitated.

This woman knew her husband. She knew that if he was yelling at her like this, it was paramount she should do what he said. Her trust, which came from knowing his character, who he is at his core, allowed her to obey without question, and her life was saved. In case you're wondering, they both were able to walk away from the accident.

In our earlier story about Mary, the mother of Jesus, we see the difference between knowing and knowing about reflected in the lives of Mary and Zechariah. Mary knew her God and that knowing enabled her to say yes without hesitation. But even though Zechariah knew a lot about God and had served God for many years, He allowed doubt and disillusionment to cloud his view of God, and it left him unable to fully trust.

*Do you know God intimately or do you just know about Him? Explain.*

*Are you a worrier, control freak, doubter, complainer, plagued with anxiety? What could these heart attitudes reflect about your belief in God?*

# Dangerous Living = Radical Obedience

If we do not know God, we won't trust Him, and if we don't trust Him, we will never dare to live a dangerous life for God. We will always settle for the comfortable and mediocre.

Daring to live dangerously starts with knowing our God. **True, unquestioning obedience only happens in the heart of a follower who truly knows her God.**

But so often we get it backward. We attempt to obey God without trusting, and we try to trust without knowing Him. And we wonder why we're stuck. Why can't we live in victory?

At the heart of every man-made religion is this idea: we must work our way to God. But Jesus came to show us those ways will always fail. It isn't about what we do, it's about what has been done for us (Ephesians 2.8–9). God sent Jesus to restore our broken relationship with Him. He gave us His Word, so we might know Him and live in relationship with Him now.

**Trust and obedience are born out of our relationship with God.** Keeping the rules does not make a relationship. It is just an empty religion. An intimate relationship with God sets Christianity apart from every other religion in the world.

**We will never be able to dare to live dangerously for God until we trust Him, and we will never fully trust Him until we truly know Him.**

# DAY 3
# DIG DEEPER INTO THE STORY

## JOHN 10.1–5, 14–15, 27–30

*"I tell you the truth, anyone who sneaks over the wall of a sheepfold, rather than going through the gate, must surely be a thief and a robber! ²But the one who enters through the gate is the shepherd of the sheep. ³The gatekeeper opens the gate for him, and the sheep recognize his voice and come to him. He calls his own sheep by name and leads them out. ⁴After he has gathered his own flock, he walks ahead of them, and they follow him because they know his voice. ⁵They won't follow a stranger; they will run from him because they don't know his voice.*

*¹⁴I am the good shepherd; I know my own sheep, and they know me, ¹⁵just as my Father knows me and I know the Father. So, I sacrifice my life for the sheep.*

*²⁷My sheep listen to my voice; I know them, and they follow me. ²⁸I give them eternal life, and they will never perish. No one can snatch them away from me, ²⁹for my Father has given them to me, and he is more powerful than anyone else. No one can snatch them from the Father's hand. ³⁰The Father and I are one."*

## NOTES & OBSERVATIONS

Refer to page 8 for guidance on how to dig deeper into the story.

*What does Jesus say at the beginning of this passage?*

*Why would Jesus start off by saying this? What is it He wants His followers to know?*

**Note:** The first paragraph gives physical description of shepherd and sheep. The last two paragraphs are the spiritual comparison. So let's first look at the physical first then the spiritual.

## Physical

1.   What does the shepherd do for the sheep?

2.   How do the sheep know their shepherd?

3.   How does a sheep follow a shepherd?

Imprinting: a rapid learning process that takes place early in the life of a social animal (such as a goose) and establishes a behavior pattern (such as recognition of and attraction to its own kind or a substitute)[8]

## Spiritual

4.   What does The Shepherd do for the sheep?

5.   What is the result of knowing and following the Shepherd?

6.   Are you one of His sheep?

---

8 Merriam-Webster online dictionary, https://www.merriam-webster.com/dictionary/imprinting.

Amassing a vast amount of knowledge of God and His Word, checking the boxes, and doing all the right things, doesn't make you a sheep.

Have you ever invited Christ into your life, to wash away your sins and make you right with Him, in order to have a relationship with Him?

*For everyone has sinned;* **we all fall short of God's glorious standard.** *Yet God, in his grace, freely makes us right in his sight. He did this through* **Christ Jesus when he freed us from the penalty for our sins.** *For God presented Jesus as the sacrifice for sin.* **People are made right with God when they believe that Jesus sacrificed his life, shedding his blood.** (Romans 3.23–25)

If you don't know for sure if you are one of His sheep, now is the time to make sure. You can do it right where you are. You might want to tell God something like this:

"God, I've done things that have hurt You and separated You from me. I'm sorry. Will You forgive my sins and come into my life? I want to have a personal intimate relationship with You. I want You to direct my life. I want to know You. Thank You for making this possible through Jesus's death and resurrection. It's in Jesus's name I say this prayer, amen."

Praying this prayer isn't about getting the "magic ticket" to heaven when you die. It is about placing your faith and trust in Jesus alone for your whole life, not just your eternal destination.

If this prayer reflects what is truly in your heart . . . a desire for Jesus to invade your life and take His rightful place, then you are now part of the family! You're God's daughter, and heaven is throwing a party for you right now (see Luke 15.10)!

Look at what the Apostle Paul says about you now, "You have not received a spirit that makes you fearful slaves. Instead, you received God's Spirit when he adopted you as his own children. Now we call him, 'Abba, Father.' For **his Spirit joins with our spirit to affirm that we are God's children**" (Roman 8.15–16).

If you are wondering if God really gave you His spirit, as He said He would, I encourage you to ask Him to affirm in your heart that you are His and allow His Spirit to confirm with your spirit that you are His beloved child.

If you prayed this prayer, I encourage you to tell someone else what God has done in your life and invite them to step into an intimate relationship with God. Will you email me, **kristihuseby@gmail.com**? I would love to know and to help you get connected with other followers of Jesus so you can continue to grow and be encouraged.

7. Do you know the Good Shepherd or have you settled for just knowing *about* Him? Have you been busy just going through the motions, checking the list? Do you have an intimate, love relationship with the God who gave His life for you, so that you might truly KNOW Him? Do you want a relationship with Him?

Recently I was watching *The World's Toughest Race.* It's a fascinating glimpse into the courage and fortitude of the human spirit. One of the men on the race told a very poignant story about his dad.

He shared how when he was a little kid, he and his dad would be out hiking in the woods in the middle of the night, and all around them were mountain lions and bears. He was terrified. But then he said he would put his hand in his dad's pocket, and he knew he would be okay. "I was safe."

This child wasn't any safer by putting his hand in his father's pocket. But this action reminded him of what he knew to be true: his dad would protect him at all cost, and he was safe.

Do you KNOW your heavenly Father like that? Will you put your hand in the pocket of your Father and dare to live dangerously for Him, knowing you are safe?

Consider doing this: Close your eyes and picture Jesus sitting next to you and pour out your heart to Him. Speak out loud or write your outpouring in a journal, because giving voice to our thoughts often leads to clarity and understanding. Start again to KNOW your God, because knowing leads to trusting and trusting to dangerous living!

# DAY 4
# PAUSE AND REFLECT ON THE STORY

*Be **still**, and **know** that I am God!*

—Psalm 46.10

Don't rush through this time.

*Be still.* You won't be able to hear His whispers if you haven't quieted your heart and calmed your mind. *And know.* Only then will you know who God says He is.

How has God spoken to you regarding what you have studied and read in Chapter 2?

What convicted or challenged you?

What encouraged you?

**Copy down the following verses in the space provided.** As you write these verses, insert your name in place of Jacob, Israel, and in some of the "you" pronouns, and think about what is being said.

*But now, O Jacob, listen to the LORD who created you. O Israel, the one who formed you says, "Do not be afraid, for I have ransomed you. I have called you by name; you are mine. When you go through deep waters, I will be with you. When you go through rivers of difficulty, you will not drown. When you walk through the fire of oppression, you will not be burned up; the flames will not consume you. For I am the Lord, your God, the Holy One of Israel, your Savior.*

*Isaiah 43.1–3*

1.   Who does God say He is, in these verses?

2.   What's the command?

3.   What does He promise?

4.   What does He not promise?

**Write out a prayer to your Heavenly Fatherand sign it, "Your beloved daughter, _____.**

# DAY 5
# DARE TO LIVE THE STORY
## *Carol*

When she prays, it feels as if this small but mighty woman of God is ushering you into the very throne room of heaven. The strength and authority with which she prays, leaves you wanting more—more of God, more understanding of who He is, more of this deep personal intimacy she clearly enjoys with her heavenly Father.

But it wasn't always like this, in fact for a good part of her life, she kept God at arm's length. This deep, intimate relationship with God would not come until many years later.

Carol grew up in Malaysia with an abusive, alcoholic father and a mother who was unable to show her the love she craved. She needed love like she needed air to breathe, but for her it was nowhere to be found. Until one day, as a fourteen-year-old, she heard the words from John 3.16: *"For God so loved the world, that He gave his one and only Son, that whoever believes in Him shall not perish but have eternal life"* (NIV).

*Could this really be true? Is this the love I've been looking for?* This unloved teenage girl decided to give God a chance. She told Him, "If this love is true, then I want it.

Jesus, if you are all that love, then come into my heart." And He did.

Carol didn't know much about God, but she had seen missionaries who had exemplified God's love. So she began to pray that God would give her a missionary to love her here on earth.

God sent Bala, a Sri Lankan man who loved Jesus. They were married in 1969 and began a life of serving God together in Malaysia. He was the kind of husband she had always dreamed of . . . he loved her, mentored her, protected her, and it wasn't long before he began occupying the space she had once reserved for God alone. Her world became Bala. Her life was Bala. Her joy was Bala. He was everything to her.

They moved to the United States so that Bala could go to seminary. Even though it was a difficult move, as they traded the warmth of Malaysia for the harsh winters of Chicago, they knew they were right where God wanted them to be.

Their marriage was flourishing. They were experiencing the blessings of God . . . until everything came to a screeching halt, and life as they knew it would never be the same again.

August 2, 1990, was a day Carol would never forget. It was not only Bala's birthday, it was the day they learned he had leukemia.

This "earthquake" shook her to the core and began a shift in the terrain of her faith. *How could you do this to us, God, after all we've done for You? All the sacrifices and service, and in return You do this to us? I thought You loved me.*

The treatment, the bone marrow transplant, and all that it entailed left Bala emotionally empty. It changed him, and he had nothing left to give. He could no longer meet Carol's emotional needs. And a tiny seed of bitterness toward her husband and her heavenly Father took root deep in her heart.

Despite the cancer that had invaded their lives, Carol continued to minister to women. Helping them walk through the process of inner healing. Then the second earthquake shook the very foundations of her soul.

Four women whom she had cared for, sacrificially loved, and walked through life with, each turned on her separately. They did not like the counsel she had given them, so they began a campaign of spreading lies about her. The pain of it all cut like a knife deep into her heart. *How could they do this to me, after all I've done for them? And even more . . . How could God allow this after*
*everything I've done for Him, after all I've sacrificed? Why didn't He stand up for her? Why didn't He have her back?*

"I'm done!" she yelled at God. "I quit. There's the door, and don't let it hit you on the way out!"

She still looked the same on the outside. She went to church. Sang the songs. Said the token prayer and knew the right words to say when someone asked. She looked good on the outside but inside it was a completely different story. What she knew about God didn't make sense to her anymore. She felt deceived. She had no private, personal prayer life and no relationship with Him. It was just a tattered religion she continued to cling to. And the tiny seed of bitterness she had allowed to take root during Bala's battle with cancer grew into a full-blown weed.

For eight long years the battle raged inside her; the bitterness grew, and the anger simmered just below the surface.

One day, alone in her house, she heard God's voice: "I'm not happy with you. Your heart is so far from me that I can't use you. You need to forgive; forgive your husband, and forgive these women who have hurt you so deeply. And you need to apologize for your own attitude and actions toward them." She began to sob, but she just couldn't let go of the hurt. "It's not fair. How can You ask me to forgive them? How can You ask me to apologize when they're the ones who have done me wrong? What about them?"

For five more months she continued to wrestle with God. She refused to do what He was asking, but even in the refusal she felt His quiet, persistent love. Over and over He would speak to her soul, *"I understand your feelings but I'm not letting you go. You have to let Me reach your heart again."*

She would feel His gentle nudges as she folded the laundry, made dinner, and cared for her children. *"You have to forgive your husband for not being able to give to you emotionally. I understand what you're carrying in your heart, and I love you. I still love you."*

Through all the sorrow and all the pain she continued to hear His love for her. *"My love is enough for you. You don't need any other love—whether it's emotional, physical, relational—you don't have to look to anyone else besides me. I am all you need."*

Through God's persistent prodding, she finally cracked opened the door of her heart.

She was finally willing to say, "If this is what You want, I will do it. I will embrace this love and I will trust that it is enough for me."

She knew what she had to do . . . asking for forgiveness from her husband and the women who had hurt her so deeply brought a healing in her heart she never dreamed possible. She was finally set free. The weed of bitterness that had flourished in her heart was yanked up by its roots and died that day. She was free. Free to enjoy a personal, intimate relationship with the Lover of her soul.

It was no longer a shallow religion she was pursuing or a list of dos and don'ts but a deeply rooted relationship with the God of the universe. Knowing Him became her quest; seeing who He said He was in the pages of His Word, sitting still and listening to His gentle whispers, claiming His promises, and pouring her heart out to Him.

Her whole life changed. Romans 8.1–2 became an anchor for her soul: *"So now there is no condemnation for those who belong to Christ Jesus. And because you belong to him, the power of the life-giving Spirit has freed you from the power of sin that leads to death."*

Carol is free. Free to love the way God wants her to love. Before the leukemia and the betrayals and her heart change, she had this insatiable need to prove herself to others, but now all that has changed. It's what God thinks that matters most. If He was willing to see the ugly in her soul, the nasty weeds growing there, and still love her and want her, then she knows, He is all she needs.

Carol's new path hasn't been easy. Becoming serious with God has often been a lonely journey. She has been misunderstood and mistreated. Close friendships have been hard to find. But deep inside, she knows she has a true Friend, a Father who will never fail her. She knows that her relationship with Christ is her power source, and the Holy Spirit is talking to God the Father for her, even when she doesn't have the words to pray. How amazing is that?

Every day her faith gets stronger in the little and the big things, in the scary things and in the things that bring her joy. Carol knows Jesus is right there with her and nothing will ever separate her from the love of God.

Because of her obedience and passion to know God more and more, this once bitter and angry woman now dares to live dangerously for God. For twenty-five years, she and her husband have traveled four to five times a year to Southeast Asia for ministry. Carol's life has impacted the lives of hundreds of women throughout Asia. Even at the age of seventy, Carol continues to travel and love on hurting women, speaking truth and love into their lives.

Carol knows her God, and because she knows Him, she's able to trust Him and she is daring to follow. She has personally experienced the Lord's goodness, and she doesn't want anything else.[9]

He is all she needs.

## What About Us?

Is your life defined by an intimate relationship with God, or is it defined by a religion you are practicing? What is one thing you will do today to begin to know your Creator better?

*For your Creator will be your husband;*
*the LORD of Heaven's Armies is his name!*
*He is your Redeemer, the Holy One of Israel,*
*the God of all the earth.*
—ISAIAH 54.5

---

9 Story used by permission.

# My prayer for you

I ask "God, the glorious Father of our Lord Jesus Christ, to give _____

spiritual wisdom and insight so that you might **grow in your knowledge of God**.
I pray that your heart will be flooded with light so that you, _____

(insert name)

can understand the confident hope he has given to those He called—His holy people
who are His rich and glorious inheritance."

(Prayer based on Ephesians 1.17–18)

# Will you dare to live dangerously and know your God?

*Week 3*

# DARE TO DIVE INTO THE DEEP

*"If you can't see the sun you will be impressed with a street light. If you've never felt thunder and lightning, you'll be impressed with fireworks. And if you turn your back on the greatness and majesty of God you'll fall in love with a world of shadows and short-lived pleasures."*

—JOHN PIPER[10]

ABBA FATHER, WE ARE SO EASILY SATIFISIED WITH TRINKETS AND BAUBLES, instead of the riches of your Kingdom. Too often we settle for a shallow religion and short-lived pleasures, rather than diving into the deep with You. Give us the desire to thirst for more of You. Unsettle us for what unsettles You, and give us eyes to see Your Truth. May we love You more deeply and follow You more wholly. Amen.

10 John Piper, "The Curse of Careless Worship", (Sermon, November 1, 1987) 2013 Desiring God Foundation, **www. desiringGod.org.**

# DAY 1
# AN ANCIENT STORY
## *The Samaritan Woman*

It was another day in another man's bed. Thankfully, he had left early, and she was granted a few stolen moments alone. As she lay on the tattered mat, she felt the sun's rays, warm on her face. If only it would melt her frozen heart.

She refused to open her eyes. She wanted just a few more moments before she had to face the reality of her day. *Maybe if I just keep my eyes closed long enough, things will be different.* Maybe last night had been just a terrible nightmare and she would wake up to find she was loved, wanted, and cherished.

But she knew it wasn't true. It was just the foolish hope of a desperate girl.

Her life was a shattered mess. She had left pieces of herself in every bed she slept in, with every new man she gave her body to.

Once, long, long ago, she had been like one of the clay vessels she carried to the well every day. Unbroken. Looking back now, she could pinpoint almost to the day when she began to see the cracks. It was the day her first marriage fell apart; the day her husband, in a fit of rage, threw a piece of pottery at her and yelled, "You disgust me. I'm done."

The wounds cut deep into her heart and left her bleeding and broken. With every consecutive marriage and failure, the cracks grew. *You're not enough. You'll never be enough.* The thought tormented her day and night.

Her friends had fallen away. Even her family had turned their backs on her, despising the woman she had become.

She was just an empty shell—the walking dead.

It felt like she had been living in this desert for years on end, a constant raging thirst clawing at her throat.

She thought about all the perceived oases she had stumbled upon in her god-forsaken desert of a life. With each new relationship, she convinced herself this would be the one that would quench her thirsty soul, only to discover, every single one was just a mirage.

Hope, love, and meaning—it was what each man promised but never delivered, and each encounter was like trying to grab the flame of a candle. It only left her burned and forever scarred. Empty promises and fleeting hope always seemed to disappear whenever she got close enough to touch. This was her life. This was all she would ever know. Disappointment. Disillusionment. Emptiness. Unquenchable thirst.

*Enough brooding for one day*, she thought.

Gathering the tattered remnants of her heart, she lifted her body off the mat.

The sun was high in the sky, a brilliant ball of light, its scorching rays now beating down on her as she made her way to the well. No one would be there and for that she was thankful. She just couldn't face the condemning looks, the turning of the heads when they would catch a glimpse of her.

She stopped suddenly. Someone was sitting by the well. *Should I turn around and leave? I just can't face another person right now.*

But the need for water, surpassed her desire to flee, so she continued.

As she walked closer, she realized the person was a man, and not a Samaritan man . . . but a Jew! Jews never traveled this way through Samaria. What could he be doing here? Jews were so hypervigilant about not associating with Samaritans. They acted like they would catch the plague just by walking on Samaritan land. *And heaven forbid, he have any physical contact with a lowly Samaritan, much less a woman!*

So why was this Jewish man sitting at a Samaritan well? And why was he here now, in the heat of the day, when no one came to the well?

"Please could you give me a drink of water?" the man asked.

*Is he talking to me?*

"Sir," she hesitantly replied, "why are you, a Jewish man, asking me, a Samaritan woman, for a drink?"

"If you only knew the gift God has for you and who you are speaking to, you would ask me, and I would give you living water."

His words were gentle, and His eyes looked directly at hers. She marveled at this. Most men wouldn't look directly into the eyes of a woman, but He did. In fact, it felt as if He could see into her very soul, when He gazed at her.

"Where would you get this living water? You have no bucket, and this well is very deep. And besides, do you think you're greater than our ancestor Jacob, who gave us this well? How can you offer better water than he and his sons and his animals enjoyed?"

The man spoke slowly and confidently. "Anyone who drinks this water will soon become thirsty again. But those who drink the water I give them will never be thirsty again. It will be a fresh, bubbling spring within them, giving them eternal life."

A glimmer of hope arose in her spirit. This hope was different than any she had ever felt. "Please, will you give me this water? Then I'll never be thirsty again, and I won't have to come here to get water."

"Go and get your husband." The gentle man continued to hold her gaze.

"I don't have a husband." And at this, she broke gaze with the man and peered at the dirt at her feet.

The old familiar shame washed over her. He would leave now. She was sure of it, because who would choose to be around such a filthy woman?

"You're right! You don't have a husband—you have had five husbands, and you aren't even married to the man you're living with now. You certainly spoke the truth!"

*Who is this man? How does he know these things about me??*

She felt a burning deep inside her. The shame was too much. She had to change the subject.

"Sir, you must be a prophet. So, tell me, why is it that you Jews insist that Jerusalem is the only place of worship, while we Samaritans claim it is here at Mount Gerizim, where our ancestors worshipped?"

"Believe me, dear woman, the time is coming when it will no longer matter whether you worship the Father on this mountain or in Jerusalem. The time is coming—indeed it is here now—when true worshipers will worship the Father in spirit and in truth. The Father is looking for those who will worship Him that way."

*Did he just call me "dear woman"?* How long had it been since she'd heard such tender words?

"I know the Messiah is coming—the one who is called Christ. When He comes, He will explain everything to us."

Looking her straight in the eyes once more, the man announced with confidence, "I am the Messiah."

Suddenly everything He said made sense. She knew with certainty that He spoke the truth.

Was it possible, He had come to meet her? This simple, ordinary Samaritan girl who had lost all hope of ever finding someone who would truly love her. He knew the sinful path she had taken, yet he didn't judge her like everyone else did. Instead, He offered her a gift—Living Water!

He understood her thirst and He had spoken directly to her deepest need. This was Truth; He *was* truth, and she knew in that moment she would never be the same again.

She drank deep from the well of Living Water and found the true oasis for her thirsty soul. It was no mirage of empty promises. It was truth. Even now she could feel the endless, life-giving, bubbling spring He spoke of, welling up inside of her. Satisfying her deepest longings. Transforming her into a brand-new woman, healed and whole. *How can this be? Just this morning I had given up all hope of ever finding true love. Now look at me!* She hardly recognized that desperate woman anymore.

She had to go and tell everyone in her town about Him. They had to hear what she had heard. What they thought of her, no longer mattered. What they said about her no longer had any power over her. She wanted them to discover what she had found, the living water.

She left her water jar by the well and rushed into the town.

To anyone who would listen, she exclaimed, "Come and see a man who told me everything I ever did. Could He possibly be the Messiah? The One we have been waiting for?"

# Taking a Deeper Look

*In this section, it is your turn to take a deeper look at this story in God's Word and see for yourself the truth that lies within. These questions are intended to be a guide as you search for the treasure. If you don't know the answers to some of the questions, it's okay. Not knowing all the answers is not a bad thing. My hope is that it will cause you to think more deeply and explore Scripture in ways you might never have, if just given the answer.*

## JOHN 4.1–30

Jesus knew the Pharisees had heard that he was baptizing and making more disciples than John ²(though Jesus himself didn't baptize them—his disciples did). ³So he left Judea and returned to Galilee.

⁴He had to go through Samaria on the way. ⁵Eventually he came to the Samaritan village of Sychar, near the field that Jacob gave to his son Joseph. ⁶Jacob's well was there; and Jesus, tired from the long walk, sat wearily beside the well about noontime. ⁷Soon a Samaritan woman came to draw water, and Jesus said to her, "Please give me a drink." ⁸He was alone at the time because his disciples had gone into the village to buy some food.

⁹The woman was surprised, for Jews refuse to have anything to do with Samaritans. She said to Jesus, "You are a Jew, and I am a Samaritan woman. Why are you asking me for a drink?"

¹⁰Jesus replied, "If you only knew the gift God has for you and who you are speaking to,

## NOTES & OBSERVATIONS

Refer to page 8 for guidance on how to dig deeper into the story.

*What do you know about the woman in this passage?*

*What do we learn about Jesus from this passage?*

*you would ask me, and I would give you living water."*

*¹¹"But sir, you don't have a rope or a bucket," she said, "and this well is very deep. Where would you get this living water? ¹²And besides, do you think you're greater than our ancestor Jacob, who gave us this well? How can you offer better water than he and his sons and his animals enjoyed?"*

*¹³Jesus replied, "Anyone who drinks this water will soon become thirsty again. ¹⁴But those who drink the water I give will never be thirsty again. It becomes a fresh, bubbling spring within them, giving them eternal life."*

*¹⁵"Please, sir," the woman said, "give me this water! Then I'll never be thirsty again, and I won't have to come here to get water."*

*¹⁶"Go and get your husband," Jesus told her.*

*¹⁷"I don't have a husband," the woman replied.*

*Jesus said, "You're right! You don't have a husband— ¹⁸for you have had five husbands, and you aren't even married to the man you're living with now. You certainly spoke the truth!"*

*¹⁹"Sir," the woman said, "you must be a prophet. ²⁰So tell me, why is it that you Jews insist that Jerusalem is the only place of worship, while we Samaritans claim it is here at Mount Gerizim, where our ancestors worshiped?"*

*²¹Jesus replied, "Believe me, dear woman, the time is coming when it will no longer matter whether you worship the Father on this mountain or in Jerusalem. ²²You Samaritans know very little about the one you worship, while we Jews know all about him, for salvation comes through* the Jews. <sup>23</sup>But the time is coming—indeed it's here now—when true worshipers will worship the Father in spirit and in truth. The Father is looking for those who will worship him that way. <sup>24</sup>For God is Spirit, so those who worship him must worship in spirit and in truth."

<sup>25</sup>The woman said, "I know the Messiah is coming—the one who is called Christ. When he comes, he will explain everything to us."

<sup>26</sup>Then Jesus told her, "I AM the Messiah!"

<sup>27</sup>Just then his disciples came back. They were shocked to find him talking to a woman, but none of them had the nerve to ask, "What do you want with her?" or "Why are you talking to her?"

<sup>28</sup>The woman left her water jar beside the well and ran back to the village, telling everyone, <sup>29</sup>"Come and see a man who told me everything I ever did! Could he possibly be the Messiah?" <sup>30</sup>So the people came streaming from the village to see him.

# REFLECTION

Let's take a deeper look at this conversation between Jesus and the Samaritan woman. As you peruse each conversation note when Jesus is speaking about the physical and when He is speaking about the spiritual and what does the Samaritan woman focus on—physical or spiritual?

| | Jesus | Samaritan Woman |
|---|---|---|
| Conversation—drink (vv. 7–9) | | |
| Conversation—gift (v. 12) | | |
| Conversation—Living water (vv. 13–15) | | |
| Conversation—husband (vv. 16–18) | | |
| Conversation—worship (vv. 19–24) | | |
| Conversation—Messiah (vv. 25–26) | | |

**Note**: This is the first time in John where we see Jesus plainly state who He is. To most of the people and even the disciples He has been vague regarding who He is. It's intriguing to think about why Jesus revealed Himself to this broken and betrayed woman first. As you reflect on this interaction, what do you learn about Jesus?

1.   What is the Samaritan woman's response to seeing Jesus for who He really is?

*Many Samaritans from the village believed in Jesus because the woman had said, "He told me everything I ever did!"* [40] *When they came out to see him, they begged him to stay in their village. So he stayed for two days,* [41] *long enough for many more to hear his message and believe.* [42] *Then they said to the woman, "Now we believe, not just because of what you told us, but because we have heard him ourselves. Now we know that he is indeed the Savior of the world."*

—JOHN 4.39–42

2.   What should be our response be when we see Jesus for who He really is?

3.   Do we need to have all of the answers in order to share the Good News of what God has done in us with someone else? Why or why not?

4.   What keeps you from sharing your most precious treasure—the Good News that Jesus died so that we might live?

# DAY 2
# GOD'S BIGGER STORY

Utah Lake, located in north-central Utah, is twenty-four miles long and thirteen miles wide, but its maximum depth is only fourteen feet, and most of it is a lot less. It's so shallow you can walk for miles and never have the water go over your head. Because of the shallowness of the lake, it is murky and mucky. In contrast to this lake in Utah, just a nine-hour drive away is one of the most beautiful lakes in the world—Lake Tahoe. It sports a depth of one thousand, six-hundred and forty-four feet, and is twenty-two miles long and twelve miles wide. Nestled in the mountains of the Sierra Nevadas, its waters are crystal clear. Even though both lakes have a very similar surface area, their depths are what make the all the difference.

## Shallow or Deep?

For much of my life, my faith looked a lot like Utah Lake; thirteen-miles wide and an inch deep. Most people would have looked at me and thought I was in deep. I looked good on the outside, but my inner life was a murky, complicated mess. Marked by worry and fear, I controlled everything I possibly could, and harbored secret sins in my mucky heart. Rage simmered just below the surface. And my thoughts were tormented by the envy and jealousy I allowed to infiltrate my heart. This wasn't how I wanted it to be. I wanted a deep-water faith. I craved a Lake-Tahoe-kind-of-faith . . . pure and deep.

Many of us, if we're honest, have a shallow religion rather than a deep-water faith.

We look good on the outside. We seem to have a depth and richness to our faith that will stand the test of time, but at the first sign of hardship or persecution, we find ourselves doubting God's goodness, questioning His plan, and taking matters into our own hands. We control everything we possibly can, all the while secretly believing we can do it better than He can.

When our second son was three years old, we thought it was high time we throw out his pacifiers. We were dreading the consequences. He *loved* his pacifiers.

But one day I did it. I cut a hole in each one. When we were putting him to bed that night, he asked for his pacifier, as usual and

I gave it to him. He started sucking on it, then took it out of his mouth and exclaimed, in a very sad voice, "It's got a hoe in it!"

"I'm so sorry it has a hole in it, would you like to try another one?" He gladly took that one, but after only a few seconds of trying to suck on it, he spit it out and exclaimed again, "It's got a hoe in it." Then he laid down, cried for a while, and went to sleep.

Pacifiers with holes just don't work. And hearts with holes don't work either.

# Cracked Cups

Because of sin, our hearts are like cracked cups . . . broken and empty. We hate the emptiness, so we do everything in our power to keep our broken cups filled.

We desperately turn to our parents, our children, our husband, our coworker, our boyfriend, a secret lover, our boss, our pastor, a friend, a neighbor with the expectation they will be the answer to our emptiness . . . only to look down and find everything they have put in our cup—value, worth, love, appreciation, identity, everything we long for—has just seeped through the cracks. And once again, we are empty.

And when other people can't fulfill us, we turn to other things to rid ourselves of this aching void. We convince ourselves that this political candidate, this hamburger, this new carpet in my home, this volunteer work at the soup kitchen, this new promotion, this radical movement, this large savings account, this exotic vacation will finally be the one thing that will fill our cup and satisfy our deepest longings.

*What person, pleasure, or thing have you asked to fill your cup?*

*How have you expected them to fill you?*

*How did they let you down?*

We don't understand what is behind all this emptiness, we just look at our lives and exclaim, "It's got a hole in it!"

Attempting to fill our own cups and satisfy our longings will make us content to splash around in the shallows like infants, and keep us from diving deep with God. We will settle for an ankle-deep, murky religion instead of a pure, deep-water faith with the Lover of our soul.

God told His people through the prophet Jeremiah, *"For my people have done two evil things: They have abandoned me—the fountain of living water. And they have dug for themselves cracked cisterns that can hold no water at all!"* (Jeremiah 2.13).

Do you see it? They abandoned God, the fountain of *living water*; and were content with their cracked cups.

But it doesn't have to be like this. We do not have to live this way.

The answer to this brokenness is Jesus. When we open our hearts to Him, when we invite Jesus into our lives, He gives us a brand spankin' new cup, and just like the woman at the well, He quenches our thirst and satisfies our cravings with His Living Water.

## Rivers of Living Water

*On the last day of the Feast of Tabernacles, the climax of the festival, Jesus stood and shouted to the crowds, "Anyone who is thirsty may come to Me! Anyone who believes in Me may come and drink! For the Scriptures declare, 'Rivers of living water will flow from His heart'"* (John 7.37–39). *(When He said, "living water," He was speaking of the Spirit, who would be given to everyone believing in Him. But the Spirit had not yet been given, because Jesus had not yet entered into His glory.)*

When Jesus left this broken planet, He sent the Holy Spirit to inhabit every believer, empowering, comforting, and enabling them to live this deep-water, faith-filled life. He is our Living Water. He fills us full to the point of running over.

Jesus said in John 10.10, "The thief comes only to steal and kill and destroy; I have come that they may have life, and have it to the full" (NIV).

We no longer need to hold out our cups, desperately rushing from one person to the next, one moment to the next, or one thing to the next, to satisfy our deep thirst. When the Holy Spirit lives in us, we are filled and living water flows from our hearts.

Surrendering our hearts to God doesn't mean we won't return to the habit of trying to fill our cups with things other than God's River of Living Water. **Unfortunately, our propensity is to return to what is most comfortable, familiar, and safe.**

# Returning to the Familiar

When we give power to fear, self-centeredness, and the need to be in control of our lives, we block God's work. We effectively dam up this River of Living Water, and our lives become arid. We seek solace in our old habits.

Refusing to allow God to break through our dams essentially stifles the Holy Spirit's power in our lives and keeps us from living the life Jesus has for us. When we build barriers between us and God, we will never experience the freedom that comes from complete surrender. We will have a shallow, murky faith at best, and at worst, no faith at all.

Surrender doesn't come easily. Refusing to turn back to the old familiar habits is hard. Regardless of how ineffective and empty a behavior has proven to be, familiarity feels safe when we are faced with the unknown.

Letting go and daring to dive in deep often feels contrary to what is natural. It can be downright terrifying.

I'm sure we can all agree that it is less scary for a new swimmer to gradually enter the pool from the shallow end, than to stand on the high-dive and plunge in. But if a swimmer only ever enters from the shallow end, they will never know the ecstasy and freedom of pushing past their fears and jumping in the deep.

We won't accidentally slip into this daring life. The pull to settle for a shallow faith is strong. Old ways and old habits die hard. Our hearts are fickle. We are so easily distracted and in a hot second, we slip back into our familiar way of living, just like we welcome our favorite old, ratty slippers. Satisfied once again with "shadows and short-lived pleasures."

# Deep-Water Living

If we are to live in deep waters it will take intentionality and fortitude as we let God tear down the barriers that keep us from going to the well of Living Water.

**If we settle for a shallow stagnant faith, what "well" will we draw from when drought and hardships come?**

I have two friends whose husbands decided they didn't love them anymore and walked away.

My first friend, I'll call her Anne, began to question God—*Why would He allow this? How could God be good and let this happen to her?* Doubts about who this God was that she had chosen to follow flooded her mind and she believed them. It wasn't long before the doubts grew into bitterness and disillusionment. And she walked away from everything she had claimed to believe.

My second friend, I'll call her Jennifer, was just as devastated as Anne. She wrestled with God. She cried out in anguish, wondering why He was allowing this in her life when she had been so faithful in following Him.

Wrestling with God, asking tough questions of Him is not wrong but what is wrong is calling into question the character of God. That was the difference between my two friends and this was the distinction between Zecharaiah and Mary. One called into question the character of God, the other trusted even as she questioned.

Anne doubted whether God was good, whether He was as powerful as He said He was. In the end the simple fact was, she didn't *know* her God and that led to a mistrust of His character. She had pursued a superficial, shallow religion and it let her down.

Jennifer questioned God too but in all her questioning she didn't call into question His character. Because Jennifer *knew* her God and even though she didn't understand, she had a deeply rooted trust in Him that held firm in the storm. She clung to God in the difficult waters. She held firm to the truth in Isaiah 43, *"When you go through deep waters, I will be with you. When you go through rivers of difficulty, you will not drown."* (Isaiah 43.2). And believed it.

How can two people who claim to follow Jesus respond in such drastically different ways? They both went to church, were in Bible studies, and volunteered. From the outside they both looked like they had a deep-water faith.

I believe it was because one was practicing a shallow religion, and the other had chosen to live in the deep waters.

When the storms came, what they were putting their faith in became obvious. What was in their hearts floated to the surface. Jesus said that wherever your treasure is, your heart will be there too.

Jennifer knew her God. She trusted and followed with unquestioning obedience. She had forged a relationship with God that was based on the truth of who He said He was. She rested in the fact that despite not understanding what God was allowing in her life, she could trust Him. Contrast this with my friend Anne, who was practicing a shallow religion. She had not forged a deep relationship with God but instead relied on hearsay to determine what she believed about Him. This ultimately left her unable to surrender to a God she didn't know or understand.

**The wonder of God's love is this; no matter how shallow our faith is, He still pursues us. He still loves us. But He will never leave us in our shallow, self-absorbed**

**lives. He invites us to take His hand and walk into the deep with Him.**

If our faith remains shallow, we will never know the depth of God's love.

But when we dare to dive into a deep-water faith with the Lover of our souls, when we surrender to His ways and let go of our own, we drink deeply from the well of Living Water and are filled.

It is often, in the hard places where we discover how deep our faith really is—a family member gets cancer, a daughter is paralyzed in a car crash, a son comes home from deployment a stranger, a husband loses a job.

It is in these difficult spaces, that deep faith dares to trust God, even though we cannot see the way. This is where we "taste and see that the LORD is good" (Psalm 34.8). This is where we see our small mustard seed-size-faith grow large. It's where we discover shallow living isn't really living at all.

The Psalmist tells us, *"What joy for those whose strength comes from the LORD, who have set their minds on a pilgrimage to Jerusalem. When they walk through the Valley of Weeping, it will become a place of refreshing springs. The autumn rains will clothe it with blessings. They will continue to grow stronger, and each of them will appear before God in Jerusalem"* (Psalm 84.5–7).

Don't give up. Don't back down. Dive in deep. Let God grow your faith stronger as you relinquish your way and grab hold of His.

This is our confident hope—that *one day, all will be made new.* This isn't just wishful thinking, it's a sure thing.

*And the one sitting on the throne said, "Look, I am making everything new!" And then he said to me, "Write this down, for what I tell you is trustworthy and true." And he also said, "It is finished! I am the Alpha and the Omega—the Beginning and the End. To all who are thirsty I will give freely from the **springs of the water of life**. All who are victorious will inherit all these blessings, and I will be their God, and they will be my children.*

—*Revelations 21.5–7*

This is the the promise God has made to those who are His children. One day, my friend, this struggle will be over. One day we will no longer have to fight the desire to fill our own cups. This yo-yo dance with God will vanish, and we will be with Him face to face, enjoying the endless spring of Living Water.

# DAY 3
# DIG DEEPER INTO THE STORY

## JEREMIAH 17.5–8

*⁵This is what the L*ORD *says: "Cursed are those who put their trust in mere humans, who rely on human strength and turn their hearts away from the L*ORD. *⁶They are like stunted shrubs in the desert, with no hope for the future. They will live in the barren wilderness, in an uninhabited salty land. ⁷But blessed are those who trust in the L*ORD *and have made the L*ORD *their hope and confidence. ⁸They are like trees planted along a riverbank, with roots that reach deep into the water. Such trees are not bothered by the heat or worried by long months of drought. Their leaves stay green, and they never stop producing fruit."*

## NOTES & OBSERVATIONS

Refer to page 8 for guidance on how to dig deeper into the story.

*What are the two people described as?*

*What does it mean to be cursed?*

*What does it mean to be blessed?*

1. Who are the cursed? (v. 5)

2. Where do they live? (v. 6)

3. What are the three things that make people cursed? What one do you struggle with the most?

4. Who are the blessed? (v. 7)

5. Where do they live? (v. 8)

6. What doesn't affect these trees? Why?

7. What barriers are keeping you from being a tree planted by the water with its roots running deep?

8. What is one thing you can begin to do this week to cultivate a deep-water faith? Write this down. Make a specific plan for what you will do.

Write out your prayer of confession and commitment to your Heavenly Father.

**Note:** When we write something down or speak it out loud, we bring into "The Light" the things that lay hidden in our hearts that we didn't even know were there.

# DAY 4
# PAUSE AND REFLECT ON THE STORY

*Help me understand the meaning of your commandments,*
*and I will meditate on your wonderful deeds.*

—Psalm 119.27

How has God spoken to you regarding what you've read and studies in Chapter 3?

What challenged you?

What encouraged you?

**Read the following verses out loud. Copy down the verses word for word, and let them sink into your soul.**

*⁵What joy for those whose strength comes from the LORD, who have set their minds on a pilgrimage to Jerusalem. ⁶When they walk through the Valley of Weeping, it will become a place of refreshing springs. The autumn rains will clothe it with blessings. ⁷They will continue to grow stronger, and each of them will appear before God in Jerusalem. ⁸O LORD God of Heaven's Armies, hear my prayer. Listen, O God of Jacob. [Pause in His Presence] ⁹O God, look with favor upon the king, our shield! Show favor to the one you have anointed. ¹⁰A single day in your courts is better than a thousand anywhere else! I would rather be a gatekeeper in the house of my God than live the good life in the homes of the wicked. ¹¹For the LORD God is our sun and our shield. He gives us grace and glory. The LORD will withhold no good thing from those who do what is right. ¹²O LORD of Heaven's Armies, what joy for those who trust in you.*

*—Psalm 84.5–12*

**This space is for you to journal your thoughts, questions, and/or prayers regarding this passage of Scripture.**

It's so easy for our hearts to become so fixated on our pain, insurmountable problems, broken dreams, and disappointments that we forget to look for the refreshing brook God offers His children.

# DAY 5
# DARE TO LIVE THE STORY
## *Victoria*

She is an old soul in a young body and wise beyond her years. I have never met anyone quite like her. There is a depth and richness to her faith that was infectious.

I had the unique privilege of spending six weeks with Victoria, while attending an internship for Community Health Evangelism in Kenya. As the only Americans participating in the internship, our hearts were knit together in a special way during our time there.

Our thirty year age difference didn't seem to matter. We laughed, we cried, we trained and taught together, and shared many bowls of popcorn over late-night talks.

Victoria, just twenty-five years old, left a good paying job as a nurse, as well as her friends and family, to live among the Sambaru in Northern Kenya.

It took me a while to realize just how primitive it is there because Victoria laughs at the inconveniences and smiles in the face of danger, and that's no exaggeration. In one of our many conversations, she nonchalantly mentioned that one time she walked into her tiny home and found a black mamba resting in the corner after polishing off a resident lizard. *What?*

Victoria sleeps in a hammock because of the snakes. Her bathroom is a pit-latrine outside her house. (In case you might not know what that is, it's a hole in the ground—a hole Victoria dug by herself, with siding surrounding it for privacy. They have no running water, and every few days she drives the Land Rover to fill big jugs of water at the bore hole. She has a solar powered oven, where she bakes cookies and bread. The temperature stays at a balmy 100–115°F every day. Life is hard, but you wouldn't know it. I never heard her complain, not even once, about her living situation.

How does a young woman choose this way of life when so many of her contemporary counterparts are pursuing their own personal comfort? What's deep down inside that causes her to live such a radical, dangerous life for Jesus? Why is she not living overwhelmed by fear when so many of us, who live in much safer environments, are held hostage by it? What keeps her from running at the first sign of danger?

As I watched her live life and interacted with her daily, I saw why. Victoria has dared to dive into the deep with her Savior. She is in love with Jesus. She spends time with Him. God's Word is precious to her.

Often, I would see her in the back of our van reading her Bible as we bounced along on the bumpy roads. This wasn't something she did for the approval of others. She hungered and thirsted after God, and it was evident in the way she lived her life. When I read the verses in Psalms 42.1–2 "As the deer longs for streams of water, so I long for you, O God. I thirst for God, the living God. When can I go and stand before him?"—I think of Victoria.

Victoria is a runner. She loves to run on the dirt roads all around her village. One day, while running, she tripped and fell right in front of the house of a woman who openly opposed everything they were teaching and doing. In the weeks to follow she would trip in the exact same spot repeatedly. Finally, she began to clue into the fact this was not a just a physical battle but a spiritual one. She and her coworkers went back to that spot and prayed over it and her. They walked back and forth along the road and asked God to bind the enemy, not just to keep Victoria from falling but to eradicate whatever influ-ence the enemy was having on their ministry. From that time on she never fell there again.

Because she's a nurse, part of her job is to treat those in the villages who are unable to get medical care. Her supplies and med-ical abilities are limited, yet God has done miraculous things in this tiny village. And Victoria, because of her obedience, has had the amazing privilege of witnessing God's mighty hand.

Is she perfect? No. In fact, I know she would be the first to say she isn't. Does she experience hard times? Yes. Living with the Sambaru in Kenya is challenging and diffi-cult, but she has chosen to put her hope and confidence in God, and in so doing her roots have grown deep into the Living Water. It sustains her, empowers her, and gives her the courage to say yes to God and live danger-ously for Him.

Victoria would be the first to say she is just an ordinary girl. There is nothing special or amazing about her, nothing that would cause her to leave the luxuries of the United States for the hardships of Northern Kenya. But she has dared to say yes to an extraordi-nary God. And what God is doing through her is supernatural and awe-inspiring—all because her roots runs deep.[11]

---

11 Used by permission.

# What About Us?

Are you willing, like Victoria, to say yes to living dangerously for God? He might not be calling you to the deep heart of Africa, but He has called you to something, of that I am sure. Are you willing to say yes?

## My prayer for you

*"May God, from **His glorious, unlimited resources,** empower you, _____*
*(insert name)*
*with inner strength through His Spirit. Then Christ will make His home in your hearts as you trust in Him. **Your roots will grow down into God's love and keep you strong.** And may you, _____ have the power to understand how*
*(insert name)*
*wide, how long, how high, and how deep his love is. May you experience the love of Christ, though it is too great to understand fully. **Then you will be made complete with all the fullness of life and power that comes from God.**"*

(Prayer based on Ephesians 3.17–18)

## Will you dare to live dangerously and dive into the deep?

*Week 4*

# DARE TO ANCHOR YOUR HEART TO GOD AND HIS TRUTH

*"When you become so blind that the maker of galaxies and ruler of nations and knower of all mysteries and lover of our souls becomes boring, then only one thing is left—the love of the world. For the heart is always restless. It must have its treasure: if not in heaven, then on the earth."*

—JOHN PIPER[12]

Lord of Heaven's Armies, *Jehovah Sabaoth*, we worship You. You are the One who saves. You are the place where our deepest needs are met. No one can compare to You. We need You like we need air to breathe. Teach us to anchor our hearts to You and Your truth. Drown out the raucous din of this world, so we might hear Your quiet whispers. May our hearts never become bored with You. Show us who You are, we want to see You. Amen.

---

12 John Piper, "The Curse of Careless Worship," (Sermon, November 1, 1987) 2013 Desiring God Foundation, **www.desiringGod.org.**

# DAY 1
# AN ANCIENT STORY
## *Hannah*

It was an ugly cry; snot mixed with tears and the kind of weeping where you can't seem to catch your breath. But she just couldn't stop, couldn't hold it together any longer. Her heart had shattered into a thousand pieces and "all the king's horses and all the king's men," could never put it back together again.

Every month found her hopefully expectant, and with each successive month her dreams were dashed on the rocks of disappointment. She tried not to get her hopes up, but she just couldn't help it. It was a hamster wheel kind of living, as month after agonizing month turned into year after tormenting year and still no baby to cradle in her arms.

With each disappointing month, it felt as if her heart was being torn in two, until all that was left were the tattered remnants of a fractured soul.

*You're no good. You have always been a failure, and you always will be a failure.* These were the thoughts that had rattled around in her head since she was a little girl. Now they were shouting through her barrenness for all the world to hear.

She had come to this place; the Tabernacle, where God chose to dwell with His people. In her desperation, she had chosen to run to the only One she knew would hear her anguished pleas.

When she had married Elkanah, there had been so much hope for their future. She dreamed of little feet pattering around their home, tiny arms wrapped around her neck, and little lips kissing her cheek. The sweet smell of a baby after his bath, and of tender moments when only she could give what her sweet child needed. But it just hadn't happened . . . and her soul mirrored the wasteland and desolation of her womb.

Attempting to comfort her in the only way he knew how, Elkanah told her one day, "Don't be sad my love. You have me! Aren't I better than ten sons?"

Did he really think he was her consolation prize? She loved Elkanah but he wasn't better than having even one son. It just wasn't a space he could fill. He couldn't understand how lost and empty she felt. How her arms physically ached to hold a little one. He didn't comprehend the pressure she was under from all the other women in her village. *Can't he see what a failure I am? Her barrenness was all the proof he needed. I am worthless.*

And if barrenness was the bitter pill she had to swallow, living with Peninnah, the "other wife" who had all the children she wanted, was like drinking poison, and waiting to die. Only she never did. Life became a living hell as Peninnah taunted Hannah's childlessness endlessly. And month after endless month marched on, with no hope in sight.

Peninnah's persecution only magnified her anxious thoughts and reinforced her feelings of inadequacy and failure. She hunkered down behind the fortified walls of her heart, in an attempt to ward off the verbal and psychological attacks from her adversary. She could feel herself sinking down into the deep abyss of her darkest thoughts, but she just couldn't stop the descent. It was a swirling vortex pulling her further and further down into its depths.

Every year the family would make the journey to the Tabernacle in Shiloh to offer sacrifices. They would always have a special meal in Shiloh, and Elkanah would give a choice portion of the meat to Peninnah and her children. And because he loved Hannah, Elkanah would give her a double portion of the meat, even though she had no children. The compassion Elkanah showed to Hannah rubbed Peninnah's soul raw. She was filled with rage and jealousy. *How can Elkanah love*

*Hannah and not me? After all, I'm the one who has given him children.*

Hannah dreaded the time in Shiloh, especially. Peninnah was extra cruel in her mocking, and the tears would begin their descent down Hannah's face. She hated that she couldn't hold them in. Hated that she let Peninnah get to her this way. It was just bitterness upon bitterness.

This year had been no different. It was the choice-meat-taunting-crying scenario all over again. And Hannah was too upset to eat, so she left the midday meal and went to the entrance of the Tabernacle to pray and pour her heart out to God, holding nothing back.

She finally gave voice to the feelings she had secreted away for so long, and as she did, something deep inside her gave way. The floodgates opened and all the pain, bitterness, and disillusionment she had held inside emptied out into the space between her and God. The chains of fear, doubt, and shame, that held her captive for so long, were finally broken. Hannah was set free. Free to dare to make a dangerous vow to the Lord: "O Lord of Heaven's Armies, if you see my sorrow and answer my prayer and give me a son, then I will give him back to You. He will be Yours for his entire lifetime."

Hannah didn't know it, but as she prayed, she was being watched by the High Priest, Eli. He thought she was drunk because he saw her lips moving but there was no sound coming out. He was immediately angry with her for coming to the Temple this way and exclaimed, "Must you come here drunk? Get rid of your wine!"

"Oh, that's not true, sir! I haven't been drinking wine. I am very discouraged, and I was pouring out my heart to the Lord. Please, don't think I am wicked! For I have been praying out of great anguish and sorrow."

Eli realized she spoke the truth. He didn't press her for the reason she was there, he simply said, "Go in peace, and may God grant your request."

"Oh, thank you!"

She couldn't explain it, but she knew in her heart that the Lord had heard her prayer. For the first time in a very long while, Hannah felt the burden lift, and she was free. The sadness was gone, and hope had returned. She went back to the family dinner and ate her fill.

And just a few short months later, Hannah felt the first flutterings in her womb. *Oh what joy! The Lord of Heaven's Armies has heard my prayer.*

Hannah gave birth to a beautiful baby boy, whom she named Samuel. When it came time to go to Shiloh for the annual sacrifice, Hannah told Elkanah, "You go on without me. I won't go until Samuel is weaned, and then we will take him to the temple to serve the Lord permanently, as I promised."

Elkanah knew how much Hannah loved this little son of theirs. He knew how long she had waited and what sorrow she had experienced. Could she do it? Could she really give up this son of hers?

"Stay here for now, Hannah, and may the Lord help you keep your promise."

When Samuel was weaned, Hannah and Elkanah brought Samuel to the Temple, along with their yearly sacrifice.

When Hannah saw Eli, she asked, "Sir, do you remember me? I am the very woman who, several years ago, was praying to the Lord. I asked the Lord to give me this boy, and he answered my prayer. Now I have brought him here to this temple. I am giving him to the Lord, and he will belong to Him for his whole life."

As they traveled home, Hannah's heart ached for the son she had left behind, but it was a good ache. Yes, she would miss him like crazy, but she was at peace. The Lord of Heaven's Armies, her king, had fought for her. What more could she do to express her thankfulness than to keep her promise? He was her hope. He was her salvation. He had patched up her shattered heart and made her whole again, when no one else could.

# Taking a Deeper Look

*In this section, it is your turn to take a deeper look at this story in God's Word and see for yourself the truth that lies within. These questions are intended to be a guide as you search for the treasure. If you don't know the answers to some of the questions, it's okay. Not knowing all the answers is not a bad thing. My hope is that it will cause you to think more deeply and explore Scripture in ways you might never have, if just given the answer.*

## 1 SAMUEL 1.1–28

There was a man named Elkanah who lived in Ramah in the region of Zuph in the hill country of Ephraim. He was the son of Jeroham, son of Elihu, son of Tohu, son of Zuph, of Ephraim. ²Elkanah had two wives, Hannah and Peninnah. Peninnah had children, but Hannah did not.

³Each year Elkanah would travel to Shiloh to worship and sacrifice to the LORD of Heaven's Armies at the Tabernacle. The priests of the LORD at that time were the two sons of Eli—Hophni and Phinehas. ⁴On the days Elkanah presented his sacrifice, he would give portions of the meat to Peninnah and each of her children. ⁵And though he loved Hannah, he would give her only one choice portion because the LORD had given her no children. ⁶So Peninnah would taunt Hannah and make fun of her because the LORD had kept her from having children. ⁷Year after year it was the same—Peninnah would taunt Hannah as they went to the Tabernacle. Each time, Hannah would be reduced to tears and would not even eat.

## NOTES & OBSERVATIONS

Refer to page 8 for guidance on how to dig deeper into the story.

*What do you observe in Hannah's pleas to God?*

*Who does Hannah turn to when her feelings overwhelm her? Who doesn't she turn to?*

*8"Why are you crying, Hannah?" Elkanah would ask. "Why aren't you eating? Why be downhearted just because you have no children? You have me—isn't that better than having ten sons?"*

## HANNAH'S PRAYER FOR A SON

*9Once after a sacrificial meal at Shiloh, Hannah got up and went to pray. Eli the priest was sitting at his customary place beside the entrance of the Tabernacle. 10Hannah was in deep anguish, crying bitterly as she prayed to the LORD. 11And she made this vow: "O LORD of Heaven's Armies, if you will look upon my sorrow and answer my prayer and give me a son, then I will give him back to you. He will be yours for his entire lifetime, and as a sign that he has been dedicated to the LORD, his hair will never be cut."*

*12As she was praying to the LORD, Eli watched her. 13Seeing her lips moving but hearing no sound, he thought she had been drinking. 14"Must you come here drunk?" he demanded. "Throw away your wine!"*

*15"Oh no, sir!" she replied. "I haven't been drinking wine or anything stronger. But I am very discouraged, and I was pouring out my heart to the LORD. 16Don't think I am a wicked woman! For I have been praying out of great anguish and sorrow."*

*17"In that case," Eli said, "go in peace! May the God of Israel grant the request you have asked of him."*

<sup>18</sup>*"Oh, thank you, sir!" she exclaimed. Then she went back and began to eat again, and she was no longer sad.*

## SAMUEL'S BIRTH AND DEDICATION

<sup>19</sup>*The entire family got up early the next morning and went to worship the L*ORD *once more. Then they returned home to Ramah. When Elkanah slept with Hannah, the L*ORD *remembered her plea,* <sup>20</sup>*and in due time she gave birth to a son. She named him Samuel, for she said, "I asked the L*ORD *for him."*

<sup>21</sup>*The next year Elkanah and his family went on their annual trip to offer a sacrifice to the L*ORD *and to keep his vow.* <sup>22</sup>*But Hannah did not go. She told her husband, "Wait until the boy is weaned. Then I will take him to the Tabernacle and leave him there with the Lord permanently."*

<sup>23</sup>*"Whatever you think is best," Elkanah agreed. "Stay here for now, and may the L*ORD *help you keep your promise." So she stayed home and nursed the boy until he was weaned.*

<sup>24</sup>*When the child was weaned, Hannah took him to the Tabernacle in Shiloh. They brought along a three-year-old bull for the sacrifice and a basket of flour and some wine.* <sup>25</sup>*After sacrificing the bull, they brought the boy to Eli.* <sup>26</sup>*"Sir, do you remember me?" Hannah asked. "I am the very woman who stood here several years ago praying to the L*ORD. <sup>27</sup>*I asked the L*ORD *to give me this boy, and he has granted my request.* <sup>28</sup>*Now I am giving him to the L*ORD, *and he will belong to the L*ORD *his whole life." And they worshiped the Lord there.*

# REFLECTION

When Hannah prays, she calls on *Jehovah Sabaoth* (meaning the Lord of Heaven's armies) to hear her prayer and answer. There are many other names of God, *Jehovah Rapha* (the God who heals), *Jehovah Jireh* (the God who will provide), *Jehovah Roi* (the God who sees) that we might expect her to use but she didn't. It's intriguing to think about why Hannah used this specific name of God in her time of trouble.

1.  What might Hannah have been feeling when she used the name *Jehovah Sabaoth*?

2.  How do you think Hannah was able to keep her promise and let go of her son?

*Then Hannah prayed:*

*"My heart rejoices in the LORD! The LORD has made me strong. Now I have an answer for my enemies; I rejoice because you rescued me. ²No one is holy like the LORD! There is no one besides you; there is no Rock like our God. ³Stop acting so proud and haughty! Don't speak with such arrogance! For the LORD is a God who knows what you have done; he will judge your actions. ⁴The bow of the mighty is now broken, and those who stumbled are now strong. ⁵Those who were well fed are now starving, and those who were starving are now full. The childless woman now has seven children, and the woman with many children wastes away. ⁶The LORD gives both death and life; he brings some down to the grave but raises others up. ⁷The LORD makes some poor and others rich; he brings some down and lifts others up. ⁸He lifts the poor from the dust and the needy from the garbage dump. He sets them among princes, placing them in seats of honor. For all the earth is the LORD's, and he has set the world in order. ⁹He will protect his faithful ones, but the wicked will disappear in darkness. No one will succeed by strength alone. ¹⁰Those who fight against the LORD will be shattered. He thunders against them from heaven; the LORD judges throughout the earth. He gives power to his king; he increases the strength of his anointed one."*

—1 SAMUEL 2.1–10

3.   What does Hannah say about God?




4.   What does this prayer reveal about Hannah's faith and understanding of God?

# DAY 2
# GOD'S BIGGER STORY

*I'm newly married. I should be happy. But I'm not. What is this darkness that has invaded my soul and forced me down into this dungeon? I hate where I am. Why can't I crawl out of this pit? Will it be like this forever?*

I had dreamed of being married ever since I was a little girl. God had given me the man of my dreams, so why was I in this horrible place?

It started just weeks after we were married. We had spent three months apart before the wedding. He was in Michigan, and I was in California. We were so happy to finally be together. The wedding was beautiful despite the 105-degree temps outside and no air-conditioning inside. The honeymoon was wonderful.

And we were excited to settle into our new home and start life together.

I'm one of those weird people who like change. So I thrived on all the changes that came my way during my growing up years. So much to look forward to . . . spring break, summer vacation, and Christmas holidays. Graduations and finally planning a wedding. It seemed like my life had been on an ever-changing highway. So much to look forward to.

## *From Mountain Vistas to Cornfields*

We got married and it wasn't long before the realities of marriage set in. It was like I had been traveling the Alaska Highway with its beautiful mountain panoramas and breathtaking beauty, and then suddenly found myself on the level plains of Iowa with never-ending cornfields, stretching as far as the eye can see.

My exciting road trip came to a crashing halt, as I stepped into the real world of adulting.

All I could see was me. All I could focus on was how I felt. I had wanted to be a grown-up and make my own choices but now that the time was finally here, it was no where near what I thought it would be.

Disappointment and disillusionment plunged me head long into the dungeon of my soul, groveling around in my dark abyss of hopelessness and despair.

Apathy and boredom reigned. My relationship with God began to shrivel and die, as I wallowed in the muck of self-absorption. God wasn't living up to my expectations and frankly, neither was my husband. I hated where I was.

I wanted to crawl out of the pit but just had no idea how.

*Had God abandoned me? Was it just empty promises I had been clinging to? Did He hear me? Because it sure felt like my prayers were just bouncing off the ceiling. Was the hope of heaven just a figment of someone's imagination?*

*If God is real, why does He allow me to feel this way? What kind of a God would do that, after all I had done for Him?* These were my secret questions and fears rattling around in my head, but I chose never to articulate or bring them into the Light. I reasoned— *if I am a child of God, how can I voice these feelings and questions to Him? Won't He strike me dead?*

Even though my heart was so far from God, He never abandoned me. I felt like He had but unbeknownst to me, He was there, working behind the scenes in ways I could not see.

## Unexpected Encounter

Friends of ours invited us to a weekend family retreat at a camp a few hours from our home. It was there that God intervened in my life and met me in a way that would change my life forever.

It was in one of the sessions at the retreat that I sensed God speaking directly to me. I wondered how this stranger, the speaker sharing God's truth, knew me so well. This was a new experience. I had heard other people talk about this weird "phenomenon," but it had never happened to me. Until that moment . . .

The pastor took us to the passage in Lamentations 3. I was very familiar with a few of the verses in this chapter. They are some of the most beautiful verses in the Bible. *The faithful love of the LORD never ends! His mercies never cease. Great is His faithfulness; his mercies begin afresh each morning. I say to myself, "The LORD is my inheritance; therefore, I will hope in Him!"* (Lamentations 3.22–24).

But what I had never seen before, were the verses right in front these. They took my breath away as I read them. It felt as if the prophet Jeremiah was echoing my own troubled thoughts, my hidden fears and questions.

*I am the one who has seen the afflictions that come from the rod of the LORD's anger. **He has led me into darkness, shutting out all light. He has turned***

*His hand against me* *again and again,* *all day long. . . . He has walled me in,* *and I cannot escape. He has bound me* *in heavy chains.* **And though I cry and** **shout, He has shut out my prayers. He** **has blocked my way** *with a high stone* *wall; He has made my road crooked. . . .* **He has made me chew on gravel.** *He* *has rolled me in the dust.* **Peace has been** **stripped away,** *and I have forgotten what* *prosperity is.*

—Portions of Lamentations 3.1–17

Just as I was wallowing in my bitterness and disillusionment, so the prophet Jeremiah was too. I could so clearly relate to these thoughts that had sent him spiraling downward into his dungeon of self-pity. I was right there with him!

The tears poured down my face as I read these words. Finally someone had given voice to my feelings. Someone else knew. Someone else understood.

I gazed in wonder that God had not struck Jeremiah down for voicing his darkest thoughts, instead they were recorded in His Word for me to read.

I continued to read: *Yet, I still dare to hope when I remember this.* (Lamentations 3.21).

It felt as if a light was shining out from the words on the page, cutting through the darkness. H. O. P. E. It had been so long since I had dared to hope.

Jeremiah had proclaimed just a few short verses before, that all his hope was lost and yet here, he was declaring a renewed hope. *If this were true for Jeremiah maybe it's true for me too? But, where does this new hope come from? What did Jeremiah remember that gave him his new hope?*

As I studied these verses, I realized Jeremiah's hope was in the promises of God. (It was those beautiful verses I was so familiar with but had never stopped to look at the context in which they were written.)

*The faithful love of the LORD never ends! His mercies never cease. Great is his faithfulness; his mercies begin afresh each morning. I say to myself, "The LORD is my inheritance; therefore, I will hope in him!" The LORD is good to those who depend on him, to those who search for him. So it is good to wait quietly for salvation from the LORD.*

—Lamentations 3.22–26

# Faith Over Feelings

It became so clear. This was how I could crawl out of my dungeon; by doing what Jeremiah did. New hope would be found by putting my confidence in the promises of God, in who He was and not in how I felt.

You see, Jeremiah, in those first twenty verses put his faith and hope in his feelings. He believed that his feelings were truth, and inevitably they ruled his life.

**Our feelings are fickle and unreliable. Fear is a liar. Despair is a deceiver. And disillusionment is a muddler.** When we live by our feelings, we will be dragged down into the pit, stuck in the muck and mire of our messed-up feelings.

But all is not lost. When we anchor our hearts in what is TRUTH, it is possible to crawl up out of our dungeons and LIVE.

My soul resonated with this truth in Lamentations. I saw so clearly how I had allowed my feelings to dominate my life. I had anchored my heart to them and had listened to the lies swirling around in my head instead of fixing my eyes and attaching my heart to God's truth. And in clinging to my emotions, I found myself deep in my dungeon. But God was showing me the way out. He had dared to climb down into the bowels of this ugly space I was in, where my soul had long been held captive by my feelings. Ignoring the slimy walls and putrid smell of self-pity and despair, God brought the light of His truth to this enslaved girl.

Claiming His promises, believing them, living out the truth and refusing to put my faith in my feelings was how I would be set free. He was the Light I needed to follow to climb out of my pit.

What I love most about this glimpse into the inner life of Jeremiah is that he didn't hold anything back in his conversation with God. And God gave Jeremiah grace and pointed him toward truth.

*What feelings have you anchored your heart to?*

*What has been the result?*

*I encourage you to set the book aside and pour your heart out to God. Remember He is big enough to take it. This is the first step in anchoring your heart to Him.*

God didn't demand that Jeremiah stuff his feelings and hide them, instead God allowed Jeremiah to verbally vomit all over Him, then the Savior gently reached down and turned his heart toward truth. In the same way, I don't believe God wants us to hide our feelings from Him. In fact, **God is where we should go with our feelings.** It's what Jeremiah and Hannah both did.

God's truth washed over my wounded soul and brought healing and hope as I poured out my heart to Him that day.

## *Anchoring Our Heart to God's Truth*

My feelings didn't change right away. The darkness was still there, but each day I made a conscious choice to cling to the promises of God instead of my feelings. I took one small step after another out of my dungeon. It was slow going, but it was in this step-by-step journey where I learned to trust God more. I learned to anchor my life in Him and His truth and not in my circumstances, in my feelings, or in what other people might think of me.

This is what I believe Paul was challenging the Philippians to do when he wrote this:

***Continue to work out your salvation with fear and trembling, for it is God who works in you to will and to act in order to fulfill His good purpose*** (Philippians 2.12–13 NIV).

Choosing to trust in truth rather than our feelings takes intentionality and hard work. This kind of dangerous living does not come naturally. When the feelings force their way in and attempt to hold us hostage, we must resolutely replace them with truth.

Repeatedly. We need to tenaciously fill our mind and heart with the truth of God's Word, our firm foundation when everything around us collapses.

If we do not anchor our hearts to God and His truth, we will be set adrift, tossed from one feeling to another. James, challenges us to ask God for wisdom, but with the challenge he gives a warning . . .

*But when you ask him,* ***be sure that your faith is in God alone.*** *Do not waver, for a* ***person with divided loyalty is as unsettled as a wave of the sea that is blown and tossed by the wind.*** *Such people should not expect to receive anything from the Lord.* ***Their loyalty is divided between God and the world, and they are unstable in everything they do*** (James 1.6–8).

When we tether our hearts to our feelings, instead of attaching our hearts to God and His truth, it is a divided loyalty. Divided loyalty creates instability which allows us to be set adrift, tossed about on the waves of our fickle feelings. Unstable in everything.

**The world markets fear like a pushy carsalesman, demolishing our defenses and causing us to buy into the belief that we need our fear to survive.** Can you see it?

It's easy to put our faith in our feelings. It's where I feel my heart leading me often . . . but I'm convinced that Jesus didn't die so we could live in captivity to our feelings. He died to set us FREE. When we choose to anchor our hearts to God and the promises He gives, we find the freedom He offers.

Jesus said, *"I am leaving you with a gift—peace of mind and heart. And the peace I give is a gift the world cannot give. So don't be troubled or afraid"* (John 14.27).

*If God is for us, who can be against us? He who did not spare his own Son, but gave him up for us all—how will he not also, along with him, graciously give us all things? . . . Who shall separate us from the love of Christ? Shall trouble or hardship or persecution or famine or nakedness or danger or sword?*

*No, in all these things we are more than conquerors through him who loved us. For **I am convinced that neither death nor life, neither angels nor demons, neither the present nor the future, nor any powers, neither height nor depth, nor anything else in all creation, will be able to separate us from the love of God that is in Christ Jesus our Lord*** (Romans 8.31–32, 35, 37–39 NIV).

These are the truths we can stand on. They are our firm foundation, our confident hope.

When we anchor our hearts to His truth, when we put our hope and confidence in Him, our feelings no longer have dominion in our lives. And we finally have the courage to dare to live dangerously for Him.

# DIG DEEPER INTO THE STORY

## HEBREWS 12.1–2

*Therefore, since we are surrounded by such a huge crowd of witnesses to the life of faith, let us strip off every weight that slows us down, especially the sin that so easily trips us up. And let us run with endurance the race God has set before us. ²We do this by keeping our eyes on Jesus, the champion who initiates and perfects our faith. Because of the joy awaiting him, he endured the cross, disregarding its shame. Now he is seated in the place of honor beside God's throne.*

## NOTES & OBSERVATIONS

Refer to page 8 for guidance on how to dig deeper into the story.

*Who are the "huge crowd of witnesses to the life of faith"? (see Hebrews 11)*

*Why did the author include this bit about a "huge crowd of witnesses" in Hebrews 12.1? He could've just started with "Strip off every weight . . ." What point do you think he wants us to get regarding the "crowd of witnesses"?*

1.    What are the weights that slow you down in your "race"?




2.    What are the sins that trip you up?




3.    What happens to followers of Jesus who carrying "extra baggage" as they run the race?




4.    How do we strip off the weights and sins that are slowing us down? (v. 2)




**Confession:**

- Ask God to show you what might be weighing you down and tripping you up.

- Acknowledge what these specific things have done to hold you back and keep you from running the race. (Consider writing them down.)

- Claim God's forgiveness. When Christ died, He paid the penalty for all our sin—past, present and future. When Jesus, on the cross said, "It is finished," it meant no more had to be done to pay for our sins. You have already been forgiven. Thank Him and claim the forgiveness He has already given you. (Burn or tear up your paper that you've written your confession on. To remind you, you are forgiven. They're gone.)

- Walk in your restored relationship with your Savior.

5.  How do we run the race with endurance? (v. 2)

6.  What can happen to us if we don't anchor our hearts to God and His truth?

**Note**: The Amish put blinders on their horses so that they are only able to see straight ahead. This helps the horses not to be frightened by their surroundings. It's so easy for us to be distracted, frightened, and controlled by our circumstances, but when we surrender to Him, when we fix our eyes on Jesus, our circumstances no longer have power over us, our feelings no longer dominate us, and our fear no longer controls us.

7.  When times were hard, Hannah turned to God. It is tempting to run to an "easy fix" during our times of pain, brokenness, and confusion—people, alcohol, food, shopping, etc. Where do you run when times get hard? Why?

8.  How will you fix your eyes on Jesus and anchor your heart to Him this week?

# DAY 4
# PAUSE AND REFLECT ON THE STORY

*But she delights in the law of the Lord, meditating on it day and night.*
—Psalm 1:2

What has God been speaking to you regarding what you have just read and studied in Chapter 4?

What challenged you?

What encouraged you?

*You will keep in perfect peace all who trust in you, all whose thoughts are **fixed on you!** Trust in the Lord always, for the Lord God is the eternal Rock.*
—Isaiah 26.3–4

1.   What is the promise in these verses?

2.    Are there any conditions to the promises? If so, what are they?

3.    What are the commands?

4.    What is God compared to? What does this mean to you?

## Praying Through Scripture

*You will keep in perfect peace*
*all who trust in you,*
*all whose thoughts are fixed on you!*
*Trust in the* Lord *always,*
*for the* Lord God *is the eternal Rock.*
—Isaiah 26.3–4

Now use the above verses as a guide to write a prayer to the Lord.

**Lord, I adore You:** (What character qualities of God will you praise Him for from the above verses?)

*Lord, I confess:* (What sins has God revealed to you that you need to tell Him about? Remember if you are His child, He has already forgiven you. Confession breaks down the barrier that is erected between us and God when we sin.)

*Lord, I thank You*: *(How has God blessed you? What are you thankful for?)*

*Deliver me from:* (What needs do you have? What burdens do you carry that you need to lay at His feet?)

*Lord, I love You because:*

# DAY 5
# DARE TO LIVE THE STORY
## *Lisa*

SHE IS A QUIET, UNASSUMING WOMAN WHO IS happy being in the background. Beautiful inside and out, she is marked by a gentle and quiet spirit. But this gentle, quiet-spirit, ordinary woman is daring to live dangerously for God.

I first met Lisa in a small group I was leading at our church. I don't think she said anything until we were about three weeks in, but when she did, it felt like that old commercial; "When E. F. Hutton talks, people listen." This was Lisa. Every time she spoke, you could hear a pin drop in the room as we all tuned in to what she was saying.

I will never forget those first words she spoke, three weeks into our group time . . . "I fasted and prayed for my husband for a year, and God restored our marriage." It felt as if all the air was sucked out of the room.

*What? A whole year of fasting! Who does this?* It took my breath away. What kind of a woman would have this kind of dedication and commitment? My own meagre prayer life and resistance to fasting loomed large, as I listened to this soft-spoken woman. Little did I know then that God had so

much more for me to learn from this gentle warrior-woman.

Lisa grew up going to church, attending a Christian school, and doing all the "right" things. She took catechism classes and made her profession of faith, but something was missing. It wasn't until she heard Joni Eareckson Tada (a woman paralyzed from the neck down in a diving accident when she was a teenager) speak at a conference that she began to realize her need for a Savior. Joni invited those who had decided to follow Jesus to boldly come to the front of the auditorium. Shy, stick-to-the-background, teenage, Lisa knew God was compelling her to step out and go forward. With sweaty palms and a racing heart, Lisa obeyed. She gave her whole heart to Jesus that day. Her faith became her own, and she began to grow. God's Word played a huge part in her development as a follower of Jesus. Even as a teenager, Lisa could be found sitting on her bed, reading her Bible.

Early on, God was forging in her a love and passion for His Word.

Lisa married Jeff in June of 1984 and she and her husband began serving in the church together. Jeff moved from secular work to full-time Christian ministry then back into the secular world. During this twenty-year period, Lisa thought her relationship with God was strong but even when her world began to fall apart, she still didn't recognize that her foundation was crumbling down around her.

Experiencing massive changes in her life in a short space of time left Lisa reeling. She had never been good with change, and these changes brought devastating upheaval in her highly sheltered world. Loneliness set in and depression soon followed in its wake. Her feelings dominated her life, dictating her responses both to God and her husband. The shame of not being the "perfect" follower of Jesus propelled her deep into her dungeon, as she hid away the hurt.

The life she thought she had all figured out continued to crumble down around her.

Her husband, Jeff, began to question his faith, their marriage and pretty much everything else. The day her husband spat out, "I know I love you, but I don't feel love for you." is etched forever in her mind.

Their marriage in shambles, she knew they were both to blame. It caused her to take a good hard look at herself, and what she saw wasn't pretty. The need to control everything had pushed her husband away and in response to her nagging, he did everything he could to make her life miserable. It was a vicious cycle, and neither one of them knew how to step off it.

Having nowhere else to go, Lisa turned to God. She was broken and empty, and knew she could not love this man without God's help. On her knees beside her bed, she cried out to God and asked Him to show her how to love her husband.

Lisa began reading a book, she'd had on the shelf for years and never read, Stormie Omartian's book, *The Power of a Praying Wife*. The tears poured down her face as she read the first chapter. She knew this was what God was calling her to do. While reading the book and praying for her husband, she sensed the Spirit pressing upon her heart ways in which to love her husband.

It started with napkin notes. Each day she would write a note on a napkin and put it in his lunchbox. Day after day the napkin came back in the lunchbox and she would throw it away. There was no comment about the notes. Just silence. Then one day she opened the lunchbox, to find a note written on the other side of the napkin. And God began to knit their hearts back together. They continued to pass notes in the lunchbox for more than ten years.

She was also prompted to choose one day a week to fast and pray for Jeff and their marriage. After fasting and praying for nearly a year, one morning they had a fight to end all fights before he left for work. Later that morning she received a phone call from her husband's best friend. He told her that Jeff had asked to meet up, and he seemed anxious. He was calling Lisa to make sure everything was okay.

Lisa knew that if her husband had called his friend for help, Jeff must really be upset. She fell on her knees beside her bed and wept.

In her brokenness she turned to the only One who would hear her prayers. She chose to anchor her heart to God. She was honest as she poured out her heart . . . "God, I have been fasting and praying for so long and it feels like nothing is happening. Instead, we have had one of the biggest blow ups ever, and my husband is broken and hurting. I am broken and hurting."

As she prayed and poured out her heart to God, she felt the Spirit say to her, "Isn't this what you have been praying for? You have been praying Psalm 51.17 over him all year. 'The sacrifice you desire is a broken spirit. You will not reject a broken and repentant heart, O God.' Do you not see I am doing a new thing here?"

This fight to end all fights was ultimately the catalyst that led to the restoration of their marriage.

God used this difficult time to forge within her a mighty prayer-warrior's heart. Her Bible is still full of little prayer notes of Scripture that she prayed over her husband during that time.

Praying Scripture over her husband, led to praying Scripture over her children, her family, her friends. This habit of praying Scripture over people has weaved itself so intricately into her prayer-life, she doesn't even realize she's using Scripture as she prays. It is just the way she talks to God. She has learned that no matter where she is, God hears her; whether she's taking a walk, driving in the car, making dinner, or on her knees by her bed. God hears and answers in ways she never dreamed possible. Prayer is as natural and automatic as breathing.

Lisa would be the first to tell you that by no means is she the perfect prayer warrior. She has had times of desert-walking with God, where she feels far, far away. She has had times when she doesn't know what to pray or how to pray. But she continues to press on, persevering even in the dry seasons, claiming God's promise in Galatians 6.9, *"She will reap a harvest of blessing, if she doesn't give up."*

And I have had the privilege of experiencing the blessing of Lisa's prayer-warrior prowess as she has joined with me in fasting and praying for my ministry and family.

It's easy to discount her prayer valiance because it is in the quiet of her bedroom, where no one sees and no one knows, but God. But make no mistake . . . GOD IS DOING MIGHTY THINGS through His prayer-warrior princess!

He has not called Lisa to live in the heart of Africa or to speak to vast crowds of people about Jesus. He has called her to do battle in the war-room of her bedroom. She has accepted His call, anchored her heart in truth and become a mighty warrior who is dangerous to the kingdom of evil.

Don't let the hidden nature of her battles diminish the mark she is leaving on God's Kingdom. She is an ordinary woman who has dared to anchor her heart in God and His truth. The Holy Spirit is empowering her to do extraordinary things that will have a lasting impact here on earth and on into eternity.[13]

## What About Us?

How will you begin to anchor your heart to God and His truth? The first step is in acknowledging the feelings you have allowed to dictate your life and pouring them out to God.

## My prayer for you

*"God has given* _____ *both His promise and His oath.*
          *(insert your name)*
*These two things are unchangeable because it is impossible for God to lie. Therefore, you who have fled to Him for refuge can have great confidence as you hold to the hope that lies before you.* **This hope is a strong and TRUSTWORTHY ANCHOR for your soul. It leads you through the curtain into God's inner sanctuary.** *Jesus has already gone in there for you. He has become your eternal High Priest."*

(Prayer based on Hebrews 6.18–20)

## Will you dare to live dangerously and anchor your heart to God and His truth?

---

13 Used by permission; names have been changed

*Week 5*

# DARE TO SWITCH ALLEGIANCE

*God rescued us from dead-end alleys and dark dungeons. He's set us up in the kingdom of the Son he loves so much, the Son who got us out of the pit we were in, got rid of the sins we were doomed to keep repeating.*

*—APOSTLE PAUL[14]*

King of kings and Lord of lords, thank you for rescuing us from our dead-end alleys and dark dungeons. Show us how to live in Your Kingdom. We want to worship You and You alone. We confess our propensity is to push You off Your rightful throne and assert ourselves as the ultimate authority. Forgive us Lord, and teach us, as Your princess warriors, how to live in humble adoration to You our Savior and King. Amen.

---

14 Apostle Paul (Colossians 1.13–14 MSG).

# DAY 1
# AN ANCIENT STORY
## *Rahab*

"BANG! BANG! BANG!" EVERY CRASH ON THE door, felt like a punch in the gut. Her heart was pounding like a herd of horses running at full speed. She could taste the bile in her mouth. Fear always did that to her. She had known they would be here banging on her door, but she hadn't expected it so soon. Such nosy neighbors she had.

It sounded like the whole of the king's army was outside her door. She took a deep breath, attempting to still the herd of horses in her chest and forced herself to walk slowly to the door.

This was a defining moment. She was changing allegiances. Aligning herself with the untried and untested, but she knew deep down, it was right. She had heard enough to know the God of the Israelites was different. He was like no other god she had ever heard of.

She had never been a daring person. She had never done even one brave thing in her life . . . until now.

Just contemplating her possible betrayal had sent shards of fear into her heart. And now it wasn't just a possibility, she was actually doing it.

*I am a prostituted woman.* Oh, how she hated the label the world had given her. Just the word itself sounded dirty. She felt used up, walked on, and trampled over. *I am ready for a change. Ready to abandon everything and align my heart with the God of the Israelites.*

Summoning the fragments of her courage, she opened the door.

"WHERE ARE THE SPIES? We know they are with you! The King has sent orders that you turn them over immediately."

She could smell the fear. These men were terrified. And they had every right to be. They had all heard the rumors about a large group of people making their way through the nearby countryside. How they walked on a dry path through the Red Sea. How they had completely destroyed the Amorites and their kings who lived east of the Jordan river. And now they were camped just a few short miles from her city.

"Yes, the men were here in my home," Rahab replied. "But they've gone now. They wanted to get out of the city before the gates were closed. I don't know where they went, but if you hurry, you can catch them."

The king's men rushed out of the city searching for them along the road leading to the shallow crossings of the Jordan River, figuring this would be where they would try to escape. And after the king's guards left the city, the gate was closed for the night.

Rahab raced to her roof top, where she had hidden the two spies under bundles of flax.

"I know the Lord has given you this land," she told them. "Everyone is afraid of you. We have heard how you walked on a dry path through the Red Sea. How you defeated the two Amorite kings and annihilated the people. It is no wonder we are afraid. There is no doubt that the Lord your God is the supreme God of the heavens and earth. Now promise me you will save me and my family because I have given you help."

"We offer our own lives as a guarantee of your safety," the men said to her. "If you don't betray us, we will keep our promise and be kind to you when the Lord gives us this land."

"Thank you. Now rest up and I will wake you early in the morning, before the gates are open, so you won't be discovered. Don't worry, I have a plan to get you safely out of the city."

Early the next morning, while it was still dark, Rahab dropped a long scarlet rope out her window and told the men, "This rope will allow you to leave the city without being seen. Now go to the hill country and hide there three days before you continue on."

Just before they climbed down the rope, they told her, "Keep this rope hanging out your window and when we return, whoever is inside your house will be saved. If they go out in the street and are killed, it will not be our fault. But if anyone lays a hand on the people inside this house, we will accept responsibility for their death. But you must follow these exact instructions, only then will we be bound to our oath to protect you and your family."

"I accept your terms. Now go and may your God be with you."

Rahab kept watch out her window, waiting for the Israelites to appear. The scarlet rope a continual reminder of the promise. Then one day they were there, marching around the city. It was the strangest thing she had ever seen. *What are they waiting for? Why don't they just charge in and defeat Jericho?*

She watched as this large group of warriors, completely silent, except for the continual blowing of horns by the priests, walked around their city.

She had gathered her family in her home at the first sign of the Israelites. She didn't know when their rescue would take place. She had assumed they would have attacked by now, but all they had done was walk around the city and leave. And it was the beginning of the seventh day of this strange "battle" and still nothing had happened.

So she wondered and waited, the scarlet rope of hope hanging from her window. A stark contrast against the sandstone-colored rock wall.

It had felt like an eternity . . . imprisoned for seven days in her home. She had been held captive for most of her life—not physically but in so many other ways. Each man she slept with, for her own survival, was a daily reminder of the captivity she lived in. But this imprisonment was different, and the scarlet rope was a constant reminder of the hope she dared to trust. A hope that the God of the Israelites would keep His promise and rescue her.

As she watched these unusual silent warriors walk day after day, around her city, she clung to the fragile promise of strangers. *Will today be the day that I am set free? Will today be the day I step into a new life and leave the past behind?* She knew deep down; these people were different. Their God was like no other god.

While she held onto hope, her heart was filled with fear. *What if the spies don't keep their promise? What if I'm too dirty? What if they forget? What if they don't accept me?* It was tug-of-war inside of her; clinging to hope while fear threatened to pry her hands from it.

A daisy petal pull. *Will He or won't He? Will He or won't He? Will this God rescue me, or will He see me only as a dirty, broken woman, unworthy of rescue?*

This endless circling battle mirrored the one in her own soul. When would it be over?

The city was taut with fear. She could smell it. Even though they were barricaded in her home, the fear still forced its way inside.

As the seventh day of their captivity dawned, she sensed a difference. This was the day. It was about to begin . . . this new life she had been dreaming of for so long was finally here.

The noise was deafening. The house began to shake. She listened to the sounds of her world crashing down around her, as she clung to her scarlet rope of hope. As quickly as it started, it stopped. The world was still. Not a sound could be heard. For an instant, Rahab wondered if her hearing had been damaged. It was a quiet she had never known. She gazed in wonder at her family members through the haze of dust in the room.

They were safe.

Bang! Bang! Bang! It sent shivers down her spine. But this time it was different. She knew they were coming to rescue her. She was safe. Her family was safe. The fear was gone. She had dared to trust this God of Israel, and He had kept His promise.

Without hesitation, she threw open wide the door and stepped into a new life.

# Taking a Look Deeper

*In this section, it is your turn to take a deeper look at this story in God's Word and see for yourself the truth that lies within. These questions are intended to be a guide as you search for the treasure. If you don't know the answers to some of the questions, it's okay. Not knowing all the answers is not a bad thing. My hope is that it will cause you to think more deeply and explore Scripture in ways you might never have, if just given the answer.*

## JOSHUA 2.1–22

Then Joshua secretly sent out two spies from the Israelite camp at Acacia Grove. He instructed them, "Scout out the land on the other side of the Jordan River, especially around Jericho." So the two men set out and came to the house of a prostitute named Rahab and stayed there that night.

[2]But someone told the king of Jericho, "Some Israelites have come here tonight to spy out the land." [3]So the king of Jericho sent orders to Rahab: "Bring out the men who have come into your house, for they have come here to spy out the whole land."

[4]Rahab had hidden the two men, but she replied, "Yes, the men were here earlier, but I didn't know where they were from. [5]They left the town at dusk, as the gates were about to close. I don't know where they went. If you hurry, you can probably catch up with them." [6](Actually, she had taken them up to the roof and hidden them beneath bundles of flax she had laid out.) [7]So the king's men went looking for the spies along the road leading to the shallow crossings of the Jordan

## NOTES & OBSERVATIONS

Refer to page 8 for guidance on how to dig deeper into the story.

*What might have been the risks Rahab took to protect spies and save her family?*

*What made Rahab go against her peers and switch allegiance to the Israelites?*

River. And as soon as the king's men had left, the gate of Jericho was shut.

⁸Before the spies went to sleep that night, Rahab went up on the roof to talk with them. ⁹"I know the LORD has given you this land," she told them. "We are all afraid of you. Everyone in the land is living in terror. ¹⁰For we have heard how the LORD made a dry path for you through the Red Sea when you left Egypt. And we know what you did to Sihon and Og, the two Amorite kings east of the Jordan River, whose people you completely destroyed. ¹¹No wonder our hearts have melted in fear! No one has the courage to fight after hearing such things. For the LORD your God is the supreme God of the heavens above and the earth below.

¹²"Now swear to me by the LORD that you will be kind to me and my family since I have helped you. Give me some guarantee that ¹³when Jericho is conquered, you will let me live, along with my father and mother, my brothers and sisters, and all their families."

¹⁴"We offer our own lives as a guarantee for your safety," the men agreed. "If you don't betray us, we will keep our promise and be kind to you when the LORD gives us the land."

¹⁵Then, since Rahab's house was built into the town wall, she let them down by a rope through the window. ¹⁶"Escape to the hill country," she told them. "Hide there for three days from the men searching for you. Then, when they have returned, you can go on your way."

¹⁷Before they left, the men told her, "We will be bound by the oath we have taken only if you

*follow these instructions. <sup>18</sup>When we come into the land, you must leave this scarlet rope hanging from the window through which you let us down. And all your family members—your father, mother, brothers, and all your relatives—must be here inside the house. <sup>19</sup>If they go out into the street and are killed, it will not be our fault. But if anyone lays a hand on people inside this house, we will accept the responsibility for their death. <sup>20</sup>If you betray us, however, we are not bound by this oath in any way."*

*<sup>21</sup>"I accept your terms," she replied. And she sent them on their way, leaving the scarlet rope hanging from the window.*

*<sup>22</sup>The spies went up into the hill country and stayed there three days. The men who were chasing them searched everywhere along the road, but they finally returned without success.*

# REFLECTION

On the seventh day the Israelites got up at dawn and marched around the town as they had done before. But this time they went around the town seven times. [16]The seventh time around, as the priests sounded the long blast on their horns, Joshua commanded the people, "Shout! For the LORD has given you the town! [17]Jericho and everything in it must be completely destroyed as an offering to the LORD. Only Rahab the prostitute and the others in her house will be spared, for she protected our spies.

[18]"Do not take any of the things set apart for destruction, or you yourselves will be completely destroyed, and you will bring trouble on the camp of Israel. [19]Everything made from silver, gold, bronze, or iron is sacred to the LORD and must be brought into his treasury."

[20]When the people heard the sound of the rams' horns, they shouted as loud as they could. Suddenly, the walls of Jericho collapsed, and the Israelites charged straight into the town and captured it. [21]They completely destroyed everything in it with their swords—men and women, young and old, cattle, sheep, goats, and donkeys.

[22]Meanwhile, Joshua said to the two spies, "Keep your promise. Go to the prostitute's house and bring her out, along with all her family."

[23]The men who had been spies went in and brought out Rahab, her father, mother, brothers, and all the other relatives who were with her. They moved her whole family to a safe place near the camp of Israel.

[24]Then the Israelites burned the town and everything in it. Only the things made from silver, gold, bronze, or iron were kept for the treasury of the LORD's house. [25]So Joshua spared Rahab the prostitute and her relatives who were with her in the house, because she had hidden the spies Joshua sent to Jericho. And she lives among the Israelites to this day.

—JOSHUA 6.15–25

Salmon was the father of Boaz **(whose mother was Rahab)**. Boaz was the father of Obed (whose mother was Ruth). Obed was the father of Jesse. [6]Jesse was the father of King David. David was the father of Solomon (whose mother was Bathsheba, the widow of Uriah).

—MATTHEW 1.5–6

**Note**: God completely transformed Rahab's life. She was no longer a heathen prostitute but an Israelite; a member of God's chosen people. But she wasn't just a member, she gave birth to Boaz who was the great grandfather of King David and ultimately was in the genealogical line of our Savior. How amazing is that?

1.    What do you learn about God from this story?

*It was by faith that the people of Israel marched around Jericho for seven days, and the walls came crashing down. [31] It was by faith that Rahab the prostitute was not destroyed with the people in her city who refused to obey God. For she had given a friendly welcome to the spies.*

—Hebrews 11.30–31

*So you see, we are shown to be right with God by what we do, not by faith alone. [25] Rahab the prostitute is another example. She was shown to be right with God by her actions when she hid those messengers and sent them safely away by a different road.*

—James 2.24–25

After reading all the Scripture regarding Rahab:

2.    What were the results of Rahab's transfer of allegiance?

3.    How did Rahab prove her faith and allegiance had switched to the God of the Israelites?

# DAY 2
# GOD'S BIGGER STORY

"I can't do anything right. I give up!" He flung the words at me and stomped out of the room.

This was the cataclysmic moment, when I finally awoke to the fact that the problem wasn't him; it was me.

From the moment we were married, I had been trying to change my husband. I thought when we married, my husband understood it was his mission in life to make me look good. Somehow, he hadn't gotten the memo (and for that matter, neither had my kids).

## Kingdom of Me

Control was the castle I carefully built to protect my vulnerable heart. It was my fortress; a place to hide out when chaos reigned. Controlling everything I possibly could was my safe place. Needing to have everything my way and never asking for help were the soldiers that guarded my castle. Their job was to maintain the perimeter and never let anyone get close enough to see how broken and vulnerable I really was. Failure was never an option. Perfectionism was the goal and must be obtained at all cost. I rationalized my behavior; convincing myself this was

what God wanted. Perfect humans, right? *Isn't this what Jesus died for, so we could be perfect and holy?* It was a messed up and broken theology. Because ultimately what I was doing was building the little kingdom of me. After all, who needs God when they can be their own queen of the castle?

Being in control, tricks us into believing we can do a better job than God. It fools us into thinking we are free; we are our own person. What we don't realize, is **the castle we have carefully built isn't a castle at all—it's a prison.**

# The Crazy-Making Cycle

You see needing to be in control means . . . we're responsible for everything (that's a heavy load to carry). And because we are responsible for everything, worry becomes our constant companion and fear, our DICTATOR. Control is good at convincing us this is where life is found, safe and secure behind our fortified castle walls.

So even though I knew the problem in our marriage was me, I didn't know there was another way of living. Years went by, our marriage fraying at the edges. With the addition of kids, the frayed edges turned into huge fissures. I just couldn't seem to hold everything together. I was on the crazy-making cycle of fear→anger→control→worry.

Something would happen and trigger my fear. I would lash out in anger, at my kids or my husband because I was afraid, then I would attempt to take more control. And because I thought it was all up to me, worry consumed my thoughts. Around and around we went on this crazy-making cycle.

The weird thing was, I had fooled myself into thinking I was trusting God. Convincing myself that if I said I trusted God then it must be true.

James said, *"Suppose you see a brother or sister who has no food or clothing, and you say, "Good-bye and have a good day; stay warm and eat well"—but then you don't give that person any food or clothing. What good does that do? So you see,* **faith by itself isn't enough. Unless it produces good deeds, it is dead and useless**" (James 2.15–17).

Is James saying here that if you do good deeds than you can earn your way to heaven? No. What he's simply saying is, **the way you live—the choices you make—reflect what you believe.** It's not enough to just say we believe something; we must live it out.

James goes on to further clarify his point, *"Rahab the prostitute is another example.* **She was shown to be right with God by her actions** *when she hid those messengers and sent them safely away by a different road. Just as the body is dead without breath, so also faith is dead without good works"* (James 2.25–26). Rahab believed the God of the Israelites was the One True God, and because she believed she chose to protect the spies and align herself with God's Kingdom.

# A New Way of Thinking

When I began to understand, this truth from James hit me hard: **The way I live reflects what I believe.** I took a good hard look at my life. There were huge contradictions in what I said I believed and how I was really living.

I started asking the hard questions. If worry is plaguing my life, what am I really believing about God? Why am I so quick-tempered? What's driving the anger? If fear is dictating my actions, what am I believing? If I'm jealous, what do I really think is true?

I didn't like the answers!

But it was in this hard space that God began to tear down my castle walls. He demolished the false beliefs so that He could replace them with His truth.

I had become painfully aware of how my control was fracturing our marriage and everything else in my life. It was killing me. It was killing us. I was decimated by worry and fear. Most nights found me lying wide awake, tormented by my vivid imagination of "what-ifs." I hated it. I hated what worry was doing to me. I hated this anger spewing girl I had become. I was at the end of myself—a hard place to be but a good place for God to begin His work.

*If fear and worry are dictating your life, what are you believing about God's character?*

*What is a destructive behavior or thought pattern in your life?*

*What the underlying belief you are believing about God?*

# Stepping Out of the Crazy-Making Cycle

It was clear God was calling me to submit to my husband and ultimately surrender my life to Him. But I was assaulted by my thoughts: *You can't do that. Don't you know you'll be walked on, a doormat for your husband to stomp all over? Who will look out for you? If you don't do it, no one will. How can you ask me to do this?*

But I was desperate. I knew I could not continue the road I was traveling. Proverbs 14:12 says, *There is a path before each person that seems right, but it ends in death.* For so long, I thought the path I was following was right, but I could clearly see the death and destruction that lay ahead. I knew I had to make a sharp right turn.

Clearly it wasn't enough to just say, "I submit and surrender." This sin was so deeply woven into the fabric of my life, I knew it wasn't going to be ripped out by reading another book or asking my husband to hold me accountable. If this ugly heart was going to change, if my actions were going to be different, it would take a supernatural intervention. Only God could break down these massive castle walls and soften my stony, stubborn heart.

And like Hannah, I dared to make a dangerous covenant with God . . .

"Lord, if you point out **every time** I am trying to take control, I will say I'm sorry to whomever. Whether it's You, my husband, or even my children."

My part was to listen and obey. God's part was to show me my sin. Yes, it was sin. Calling it what it was, was the first step in changing directions.

In 1 John 2, the Message version says this, *"Don't love the world's ways. Don't love the world's goods. **Love of the world squeezes out love for the Father**. Practically everything that goes on in the world—**wanting your own way**, wanting everything for yourself, wanting to appear important—**has nothing to do with the Father**. It just isolates you from him. The world and all its wanting, wanting, wanting is on the way out—but whoever does what God wants is set for eternity"* (vs.15–17).

When I must have my own way, what am I saying about God's way? The plain truth is, my actions say that my way is better than His.

You can't love the Father and want your own way too— it just doesn't work. It's either one or the other. Just as light and darkness cannot live together in the same space, neither can wanting our own way and wanting God's way. It just DOES NOT work.

When I say I want God's way but then live my own way, the only person I'm deceiving is myself.

# Tearing Down Castle Walls

I was tired of living in the deception. I wanted to come clean. I wanted a new way of living. So God and I began the hard work of breaking down the walls of my castle. And I stepped into one of the most painful times I have ever experienced.

It was hard to see my sin over and over again. It was excruciating to look at the destruction my selfishness had caused in our marriage. It was incredibly difficult to say, "I'm sorry" time and time again in conversations with God, my husband, and my children.

"Sorry" never likes to come out of my mouth. Every time I know I should say I'm sorry, it's a humongous internal battle to get "sorry" out. It feels glued to my tongue. To ease the pain, I found myself saying, "I'm sorry, but if you hadn't . . ." I had to be honest with myself. **An excuse attached to a "sorry" is never true repentance.**

Saying I'm sorry was difficult because what it felt like I was really saying was, "I'm a failure." There was so much shame wrapped up in this tiny phrase. Not because it was true but because of my own pursuit of perfection. My identity was so intertwined with my performance and other people's opinions of me that I could not separate my behavior and what other people might think of me from who God said I was.

Robert McGee in his book, *The Search for Significance* says this, "Isn't it amazing that we turn to others who have a perspective as limited and darkened as our own to discover our worth! Rather than relying on God's steady, uplifting reassurance of who we are, **we depend on others who base our worth on our ability to meet their standards. . . .**

"Our value is not dependent on our ability to earn the fickle acceptance of people, but rather, its true source is the love and acceptance of God. He created us. He alone knows how to fulfill all of our needs."[15]

# Identity Crisis

Now God and I had finally destroyed enough of my castle walls to get at the real sin issue in my life. I was seeking to find my self-worth and identity in what I did and what other people thought of me. It's why I was so frustrated when my husband and kids didn't "perform" the way I thought they should. It felt as if they were shouting to the world,

---

15 Robert S. McGee, *The Search for Significance* (Nashville, TN: Thomas Nelson, 2003), 11, 19.

"Kristi is a failure!" It's why "sorry" was so hard to get out of my mouth. I was admitting I was a failure. It's why I let perfectionism stand guard at the door of my castle.

Allowing God to shine His light on the habits and beliefs that I had concealed for so long, in the deep dungeon of my soul, was extremely painful. Being stripped bare is humbling, and having old habits and patterns demolished is agonizing.

Jesus tells us, *"All who do evil hate the light and refuse to go near it for fear their sins will be exposed.* **But those who do what is right come to the light** *so others can see that they are doing what God wants"* (John 3.20–21).

As God held up his end of the bargain, so did I. This pact we made together aligned my heart to His. I began to want God's way, not my way. The Kingdom of Me was being demolished, even as the Kingdom of God was being erected.

This demolishing happened when I removed myself from the throne of my life—the seat of authority—and invited God to be King.

## Jailbreak!

When God invited me on this journey of surrender and submission, he impressed on me the need for mutual submission in my marriage, that is, I wasn't doing my part to be submissive in our marriage. I felt as if He was standing beside a jail cell, asking me to willingly incarcerate myself. Everything in me screamed, "Run the other way!"

But I was desperate for change.

As I stood in front of the cell that day, deciding whether I was going to align my heart with His or go my own way, I felt God take my face gently in His hands and whisper, "Eyes on me, Kristi. Trust Me."

As I think back to this moment, I can feel the desperation. I remember thinking,

"All right, if this is what you want for me, then I'll do it. I won't like it but I will do it. I will make my vow and submit to my husband and surrender to You by walking into this cell, because I don't see any other way."

A feeling of dread washed over me, as God slammed shut the door. The boom of the closing door physically assaulted me as the noise reverberated all around. I grabbed the bars and peered through the small, caged window. *What have I just done?* The finality of my decision echoed. This is my life. This is what obedience gets me . . . prison.

Then I turned around . . .

A beautiful meadow with a profusion of wildflowers spread out before me. I could hear the tinkling of a brook nearby and the twitter of birds in the trees. Blue sky, warm sun, and beauty were all around me.

I. was. FREE.

Free to be the woman God had created me to be. I no longer had to live in fear and worry. I no longer had to carry the burdens God never intended me to carry.

I realized for the first time, the life I had been living was no life at all. IT WAS my jail cell. My prison. I had it all wrong. **God wasn't asking me to step into a jail cell, He was calling me out of it.** The ringing in my ears of the door slamming shut was hope, not dread. It was my jailbreak. My prison escape.

My Rescuer had freed me long ago, when I gave my heart to Jesus, but like so many of His children, I had crawled back into my jail cell and taken up residence. I hung pictures on the wall. Threw a ragged piece of carpet on the floor. Found a lamp and made the jail cell my home. It was where I felt safe. My comfort zone. I had been there so long I had forgotten what freedom was like. I had

fooled myself into thinking I was living free when I was really dying in captivity.

**Here's the unexpected and surprising truth about living in God's upside-down Kingdom . . . surrender brings freedom, dying creates life, winning comes through losing, humility ushers in power, and pain gives way to joy.** It is completely contrary to what the voices have been shouting to us our whole lives.

Paul tells us, *"Brothers and sisters, think of what you were when you were called. Not many of you were wise by human standards; not many were influential; not many were of noble birth.* **But God chose the foolish things of the world to shame the wise; God chose the weak things of the world to shame the strong. God chose the lowly things of this world and the despised things—and the things that are not—to nullify the things that are, so that no one may boast before Him.** *It is because of Him that you are in Christ Jesus, who has become for us wisdom from God—that is, our righteousness, holiness, and redemption"* (1 Corinthians 1.26–30).

## Daughters of the King

We are daughers of the KING. We are no longer slaves living with no hope but His princess warriors daring to wage war against the enemy.

As daughters of the King, will you align your heart with Him? Will you allow Him to demolish your "kingdom of me," and dare to live victorious and free, in His eternal Kingdom?

# DAY 3
# DIG DEEPER INTO THE STORY

## 1 JOHN 2.15–17

*Do not love this world nor the things it offers you, for when you love the world, you do not have the love of the Father in you. <sup>16</sup>For the world offers only a craving for physical pleasure, a craving for everything we see, and pride in our achievements and possessions. These are not from the Father, but are from this world. <sup>17</sup>And this world is fading away, along with everything that people crave. But anyone who does what pleases God will live forever.*

## 1 JOHN 2.15–17 (MSG)

*Don't love the world's ways. Don't love the world's goods. Love of the world squeezes out love for the Father. Practically everything that goes on in the world—wanting your own way, wanting everything for yourself, wanting to appear important—has nothing to do with the Father. It just isolates you from him. The world and all its wanting, wanting, wanting is on the way out—but whoever does what God wants is set for eternity.*

## NOTES & OBSERVATIONS

Refer to page 8 for guidance on how to dig deeper into the story."

*What does the world offer? (v. 16)*

*Why can't we love both God and the world?*

1.  How might you be craving physical pleasure ("wanting your own way"—vv. 15–17 MSG)?

2.  How might you be craving everything you see ("wanting everything for yourself" —vv. 15–17 MSG)?

3.  How might you be taking pride in your achievements and possessions ("wanting to appear important"—vv. 15–17 MSG)?

4.  What are you loving that is holding you captive and keeping you from aligning your heart to God, like Rahab?

5.  Think about choices you've made this past week, now consider Jesus's words in Matthew 6.21: "*Wherever your treasure is, there the desires of your heart will also be.*" Based on your answers, who holds your affections—the Kingdom of God or the kingdom of me? Explain.

***

One of my family's favorite movies is *The Princess Bride*. As the movie opens, we meet two people, Farm Boy and Buttercup. Farm Boy only says three words to Buttercup, "As you wish."

Months stretched into years, and no matter what Buttercup commanded of Farm Boy, his response remained steady.

"As you wish."

The narrator tells us that as Buttercup grew older, she began to realize that every time he said, "As you wish." he was really saying, "I love you."

When Jesus was in the garden, readying himself to go to the cross for us, He made much the same statement to the Father.

*He went on a little farther and bowed with his face to the ground, praying, "My Father! If it is possible, let this cup of suffering be taken away from me. **Yet I want your will to be done, not mine."*** (Matthew 26.39)

"As You wish," Jesus told the Father. His surrender to the Father's will demonstrated His deep love for the Father and for us! And so it is with us . . . when we live lives surrendered to Him, when we choose His way and not ours, when we align our hearts with His Kingdom and willingly say, "As You wish," we show our love for Him.

**What life will you dare to live?** As I wish (The kingdom of me)? Or as YOU wish (The Kingdom of God)?

# DAY 4
# PAUSE AND REFLECT ON THE STORY

*For He has rescued us from the kingdom of darkness and transferred us into the Kingdom*
*of his dear Son, who purchased our freedom and forgave our sins.*
—Colossians 1.13–14

What has God been speaking to you regarding what you have just read and studied in Chapter 5?

What encouraged you?

What challenged you?

Reflection: Think back to who you were before you became a believer. What was your life like?

How have you been transformed?

Read Galatians 5.19–26.

*¹⁹When you follow the desires of your sinful nature, the results are very clear: sexual immorality, impurity, lustful pleasures, ²⁰idolatry, sorcery, hostility, quarreling, jealousy, outbursts of anger, selfish ambition, dissension, division, ²¹envy, drunkenness, wild parties, and other sins like these. Let me tell you again, as I have before, that anyone living that sort of life will not inherit the Kingdom of God.*

*²²But the Holy Spirit produces this kind of fruit in our lives: love, joy, peace, patience, kindness, goodness, faithfulness, ²³gentleness, and self-control. There is no law against these things!*

*²⁴Those who belong to Christ Jesus have nailed the passions and desires of their sinful nature to his cross and crucified them there. ²⁵Since we are living by the Spirit, let us follow the Spirit's leading in every part of our lives. ²⁶Let us not become conceited, or provoke one another, or be jealous of one another.*

—Galatians 5.19–26

What characterizes each kingdom?

| Kingdom of Me | Kingdom of God |
|---|---|
|  |  |
|  |  |
|  |  |
|  |  |
|  |  |
|  |  |
|  |  |

Will it be His Kingdom or yours? Putting one foot in one kingdom and one in the other just doesn't work.

It was spring in Michigan—dreary, cold, and rainy. The dampness had crawled into my coat and made itself at home. "Could I be more miserable?" I wondered.

The idea of a daylong canoe trip on the Manistee River in Northern Michigan had seemed like a great adventure at the time. My canoe partner had only canoed on a lake, but since she had more experience than I, we agreed she should steer. Off we went, blissfully oblivious to the misery that awaited us.

It didn't take long for both of us to figure out that canoeing on a lake is completely different than canoeing on a rushing river. Before we knew it, I was laying flat on my back wedged between a gigantic tree and the canoe! Fortunately for us, there was another canoe with a couple of guys behind us. They helped us out of our predicament and sent us on our way.

But it was as if our canoe was a magnet for every fallen tree in the river! As time passed, we both grew incredibly frustrated, then things got even worse. It started to rain.

Time after time our nice friends would graciously pull us out of one dilemma after another. After rescuing us over and over, they finally suggested that we switch and one of them should go with my partner and I should join the other canoe.

I gladly put one foot in their canoe but that's as far as I got before the canoes began to separate and I fell into the freezing, mostly-melted-snow water. I came up gasping for air wondering if this miserable day would ever end.

I find it interesting how often that infamous canoe trip has mirrored my relationship with God.

When I gave my heart to Jesus, I started off with a great sense of adventure and excitement at the prospect of this new relationship with the God of the universe. But it was only a short time before I became disillusioned when life was hard and didn't work out like I thought it should.

I continued to steer my own canoe of life, getting into trouble with every swipe of my paddle. Each time I would turn to God and expect Him to rescue me, which He did time and time again. I became more and more frustrated with this yo-yo life I was leading and began to wonder if God had a different plan.

As I began to listen, God gently showed me that I wasn't supposed to steer my boat and ask for His help along the way. He wanted me to get into His boat and let Him direct my course.

I knew what I had to do. But even as I was stepping into His canoe, I found myself questioning whether I could really trust Him or not. *Do You have my best interest at heart? Will You allow terrible things to happen to me?* My fear paralyzed me and I ended up with one foot in my boat and one foot in His, which ultimately plunged me into an abyss of doubt and despair.

Praise God, my emotional bankruptcy propelled me toward change. I finally got it. He was calling me out of the kingdom of me and into the Kingdom of Jesus.

I'm living free!

Recently I heard a leader, of the largest house church movement taking place in Iran, speak. He said, "It's seems the West is under a satanic lullaby." How true.

Satan says, "Shhhh, you don't need to concern yourself with all the babies being aborted. Here's your pacificier (Netflix), just go back to sleep." "Shhhh, you can't understand your Bible, so why even try. Here's your pacifier (family, busyness, Facebook, work), night-night."

The challenge Paul gave the Ephesians is the same for us today,

> ***Awake, O sleeper***, *rise up*
> *from the dead, and Christ*
> *will give you **light**.*
>
> —Ephesians 5.14

Will you wake up from your lethargy and mediocrity? Will you refuse to listen to the satanic lullaby singing you back to sleep? Will you dare to be all in and switch your allegiance from the kingdom of darkness to the Kingdom of Light?

# DAY 5
# DARE TO LIVE THE STORY
## *Rhodess*

A smile as wide as the ocean. Beautiful white teeth against a dark background. You can't miss the joy spilling out of this woman. Ebony eyes that have seen more of life than a person twice her age. Infectious laughter that captivates the listener. Humble. Brave. God-fearing. Truth-seeking.

She sees teachers everywhere— friends, children, personal experiences, pastors, and even enemies. Always learning. But she doesn't stop there. She takes what she learns, implements it into her life, and shares it with others.

I first met Rhodess at an internship program in Kenya. Six weeks we spent together learning, laughing, sharing, singing, and living life. Two women from vastly different cultures, united by Christ. God knit our hearts together as we shared this unique time and space with one another. She from Malawi and I from the United States. Ebony and ivory. Different in so many ways and yet the same. I treasured my time with this beautiful woman and soaked up everything I could learn from her.

Every evening, after our trainings, we would head out for a walk around the neighborhood of our Kenyan home. We often shared the road with cattle on their way home after a day of grazing on the hillside. We gazed at the beautiful sunsets in the vast African sky. We walked amongst the shacks in the tiny slum nearby, all the while talking, laughing, and sharing our lives with one another. It took me a while to realize this beautiful woman lived a life vastly different from my own. I knew our lives had differences, but not until we had built up a trust with one another did she begin to reveal the challenges she faced daily.

There's a picture of the two us in my office above my desk. We took the selfie on one of our many jaunts around our Nairobi neighborhood. This picture is a constant reminder to me of the beauty of God's Universal Church, and how He is in the business of uniting every race, color, and tribe into one glorious Kingdom.

Rhodess was born in Malawi, often called the Warm Heart of Africa because of its engaging people. Malawi is one of the least developed countries in the world and is mainly agricultural. She lives in a house made of mud bricks. There are no panes of glass in her windows. Nothing to block the rain from entering her home and wreaking havoc. The floor is dirt which she polishes with a stone and water, to keep the dust down. Her kitchen is an open fire outside her home. Her diet consists of mainly vegetables and nsima (finely ground cornmeal), and meat is only for special occasions, such as Christmas.

Life is hard.

Rhodess was married when she was nineteen and has three children living and another one in heaven. A few years back, Rhodess's husband left to go find work in another village far away to support his family. But he has essentially abandoned them, leaving Rhodess to care and provide for the children and their home. She has only seen him a couple of times since he left, and very little money is sent back to her. Just recently, he has refused to acknowledge his fatherhood to their oldest child and will not help pay for his schooling, declaring, "He's no son of mine!" The pain of his decision has cut like a knife into her mama's heart. She aches for her son and feels his pain in every inch of her body.

Men abandoning their families is not unusual in Malawi. This leaves the wives to fend for themselves and their children. Many women live in abject poverty, held captive by the circumstances life has dealt them.

But not Rhodess. She has refused to succumb to the hurt and hardship of life. Instead, she is thriving. She has chosen to learn everything she can to equip herself for meeting her family's needs. She is learning new skills and isn't afraid to try new things.

In a culture, where many cannot even read and write, Rhodess has learned English and is teaching herself Kiswahili (and she's fluent in it). This is expanding her sphere of influence as she teaches others and builds a network of people who can encourage and challenge her.

Even more than learning these new skills and facing new challenges with bravery, Rhodess loves her Lord. And it's because of Him that she can face what comes her way with strength and dignity.

When Rhodess was twenty-eight years old, while attending a training school for women, she discovered who she is in Christ. She switched allegiances. No more would she let her past define her. It is God who defines her now. It is He who gives her life meaning and purpose. And she is now able to embrace the pain and hardship, as it forges in her a deeper trust and faith in her God.

As God develops this trust in her, He is filling Rhodess with a passion for others to know what she knows, to experience what she has experienced.

The easy path would be to focus on her family. To believe the hardships she has had to face are trouble enough. She doesn't need any more heartache and frustration than she already has.

Instead, Rhodess is daring to show others the way. She is teaching women of their great value and worth to God; that He created their uniqueness and beauty. And in the process she is dispelling the myths their culture has created. She is leading Bible studies and teaching reading and writing classes. She is helping women learn how to develop their own microenterprises and training them in good farming practices. She is reaching out to the elderly in her community who are alone with no one to care for them.

When I think of the Proverbs 31 woman, I think of Rhodess. She is the epitome. Rhodess often tells me that she's learned a lot from me. And while that may be true, I feel like I've learned even more from her. She teaches me what it looks like to follow Jesus with my whole heart. To surrender my way for God's way. To step out of my comfortable jail cell and live in the freedom Jesus gives.

Rhodess has discovered the truth in John 8.36, *"So if the Son sets you free, you are truly free!"* She is living proof that no matter the circumstances we find ourselves in, it is possible to live in freedom.

Rhodess has chosen to align her heart with God. He is her King. She is daring to let God kick down her castle walls as she chooses to walk in the Light and live FREE.[16]

# What About Us?

Who will you swear allegiance too?

Joshua stood before the children of Israel and boldly challenged them. *"So fear the LORD and serve him **wholeheartedly**. Put away forever the idols your ancestors worshiped. . . . Serve the LORD alone. But if you refuse to serve the LORD, then choose today whom you will serve. . . . But as for me and my family, we will serve the LORD"* (Joshua 24.14–15).

There are two kingdoms in this world. The kingdom of darkness (also known as the kingdom of me) and the Kingdom of Light. Attempting to live in both kingdoms just doesn't work. Light and darkness cannot dwell together. Refusing to make a choice is making a choice and our default will always be the kingdom of me.

Jesus said, *"You can **enter God's Kingdom only through the narrow gate**. The highway to hell is broad, and its gate is wide for the many who choose that way. But **the gateway to life is very narrow and the road is difficult, and only a few ever find it"** (Matthew 7.13–14).

Jesus doesn't promise an easy road. He doesn't tell us that if we choose to follow Him everything will go well for us. He doesn't say we will be wealthy, healthy, and safe. In fact, it is just the opposite. The road is difficult, the gate is narrow, and only a few ever find it.

But **Jesus is calling us to a life of adventure with Him.**

When we align our hearts with His, when we dare to switch allegiances, our desires

---

16 Used by permission.

become His desires. We finally have a place to belong. We are His treasured daughters. The kingdom of me is demolished and we no longer need to hustle for our worthiness because He has made us worthy.

As Joshua challenged the people, so I challenge you. Choose you this day whom you will serve. Will it be the kingdom of me or the Kingdom of God?

* * *

Lord, break down the kingdom of me . . . (What are the things in your life that are holding you hostage?)

Lord, I want the Kingdom of You, I surrender . . . (What do you need to let go of that is keeping you from living in the Kingdom of God?)

Here I am Lord, all of me. Today, I choose Your way, Your difficult road, Your Kingdom, and I relinquish the kingdom of me.

Your treasured daughter,

_____

# My prayer for you

I pray that you, _____ will be strengthened with all his glori-
             *(insert your name)*
ous power so you will have all the endurance and patience you need. May you be filled

with joy, always thanking the Father. He has enabled you, _____
             *(insert your name)*
to share in the inheritance that belongs to his people, who live in the Light. For **he
has rescued you from the kingdom of darkness and transferred you into the
Kingdom of his dear Son**, who purchased your freedom and forgave your sins.

(Prayer based on Colossians 1.12–14)

# Will you dare to live dangerously and switch allegiance?

*Week 6*

# DARE TO LIVE IN THE WONDER OF GOD

*If Christ's lordship does not disrupt our own lordship,*
*then we must question the reality of our conversion.*

—*CHARLES COLSON[17]*

Holy, awesome god—the one who hung the stars in space and spoke this intricate world into being. We confess that we have made You small. We have stuffed You into our nice neat little boxes because Your greatness scares us. Your unpredictability threatens us. Your vastness terrifies us. We ask little and expect little. Will You give us eyes to see the WONDER of You, ears to hear Your Truth, admidst the cacophony that attempts to distracts us from You, Jesus? Will you give us hearts that are smitten with You and You alone, Heavenly Father? Will you give us the courage to **unshackle You, Holy Spirit,** to do Your work in our lives? May we allow You to be the Magnificent, Glorious, Powerful, Holy, and Awesome God that You are. Amen.

---

17 Charles Colson, et. al., *The Glory of Christmas* (Nashville, TN: Thomas Nelson, 1996), 63.

# DAY 1
# AN ANCIENT STORY
## *Mary*

*It was her life savings. All she possessed. But this was what she wanted. She could hardly contain her excitement. She had so much to do today. Jesus and his disciples were coming for dinner.*

Mary had arisen early and made her way to this corner stall in the marketplace. She could hear the famliar bartering of men and woman all around her.

"Artichokes, get your artichokes here."

"How much is it for that lamb shank?"

And she smiled as the she heard the laughter of children as they played together while their mothers shopped amongst the stalls. She loved coming to the market.

She had never been to this out-of-the-way stall before. She had never had any need. This was one of those superfluous shops. Nice if you had extra money, but who had that these days?

As she entered, the shop owner's eyes lit up as he welcomed her now. *When was the last time he had an actual customer?*

There were so many jars to choose from. How would she ever find the perfect one? Her hands trembled as she picked up a jar and lifted the lid on its contents. *I'm holding*

*a whole year's wages in my hand.* She carefully set the jar back on the shelf. She took her time. She wanted just the right one. She finally found it, tucked away in a corner on the back shelf. Carefully, she removed the lid, and the sweet fragrance filled the tiny shop.

She had come to buy the very best, and the very best costs money.

Without hesitation she plunked down the large bag of coins and exchanged it for the twelve-ounce jar full of the sweetest aroma she had ever smelled. It was extravagant. Outrageous. And she thought her heart would burst with the joy of it all.

*No one will understand, but I don't care. Jesus is all that matters. He'll know. He'll understand.* This gift would tell Him everything without saying a word. Because words were just not enough to express the love and gratitude in her heart. He had become her life. He knew everything about her and loved her still. How amazing was that?

She carefully tucked the precious jar into the woven basket she carried and made her way home. As Mary weaved through the stalls in the market, she reflected on her encounters with Him.

She remembered the first time He had come to their home. She chuckled at how different she felt about Him now, compared to then.

When she first met Him, she was almost repulsed by His outward appearance. If asked, she would've said He was homely. His nose was too big for His face. His clothes hung loosely on His thin frame. He was from Galilee and nothing good ever came from there. And if that weren't enough strikes against Him, there was his motley crew of men. What an assembly of characters they were. They certainly didn't help her impression of Him either.

But then everything changed when His eyes fell upon her.

As long as she lived, she would never forget those piercing eyes, searching the depths of her soul. She felt naked, stripped bare of all pretension. But amazingly, she sensed no condemnation, only love. It was almost as if when He looked at her He began to transform. Suddenly, he wasn't homely or ordinary anymore. Instead, He was quite extraordinary, king-like.

It wasn't long before He and His friends were regular visitors to their home. She loved having Him there. She cherished the times she was able to sit at His feet and listen to His teaching. She had never heard anyone say the things He said. Amazingly, He welcomed her, a simple woman, into His circle of men. Even when her sister was angry because Mary wasn't helping with the food preparations, He had encouraged her to stay and visit with Him.

When her brother Lazarus was ill, Jesus was the one they turned to. She remembered how she and her sister Martha had sent word telling Him Lazarus was sick, knowing full well He would come.

But He didn't. Even now, she could taste the bitter disappointment. *Why? Wasn't He their friend? Didn't He care?*

Her grief was overwhelming. Four. Long. Bitter. Agonizing. Days.

Knowing what she knew now, she wondered how she could've ever doubted Him. She had been so short-sighted. Her love so fickle.

When she finally heard He had arrived, it was her sister Martha who went out to meet Him. She just couldn't. Her grief was too raw. Her disappointment too bitter.

She wasn't aware Martha had returned, until she called her name. "Mary, the Master wants to see you." Blinded by the tears of four grief-filled days, she stumbled out of the house and made her way to where He was.

What He did when He caught sight of her was forever etched on her heart. Watching the tears pour down His face as He shared in her grief, removed all the bitterness and doubt of the last four days. All her questions were answered in that holy moment. *He does care.*

And then He brought her brother back to life! To see and experience the power of this God-Man was life-changing. This was the moment she finally got it. He wasn't just a wise teacher and friend, He was God—the Promised One. Jesus hadn't just brought Lazarus back to life, He had resurrected Mary too. He had brought her into new life with Him and she would never be the same.

This was what this jar was all about. She had experienced Jesus's extravagant love. This costly gift was nothing compared to what He had done for her. How could she do anything less?

She could hardly wait to show Him the depth of her love.

He was all that mattered. He was her everything.

They had finished eating, but the evening was far from over. Mary knew it was time. Gently taking out the jar with its costly contents inside, she kneeled at Jesus's feet and removed the lid. Silence blanketed the room as all eyes turned on her. A sweet fragrance swirled in the air.

Mary could feel the stares and hear the whispered mutterings. She sensed the curiosity of some and the criticism of others. But none of it mattered.

She had eyes only for Him. The One who had made all the difference in her life. Even though there were many witnesses to this tender scene, this was a sacred and intimate moment just between she and her Lord.

Taking out the pin that held her long hair, she let her beautiful tresses fall to the floor. Slowly she poured out the aromatic oily substance on Jesus's feet. Using her hair as a towel, she tenderly wiped the oil from His feet. As she wiped, tears gently fell from her face, mixing with oil. They were tears of joy and gratefulness. Tears of love.

He was her life. He was her hope. He was her everything.

# Taking a Deeper Look

*In this section, it is your turn to take a deeper look at this story in God's Word and see for yourself the truth that lies within. These questions are intended to be a guide as you search for the treasure. If you don't know the answers to some of the questions, it's okay. Not knowing all the answers is not a bad thing. My hope is that it will cause you to think more deeply and explore Scripture in ways you might never have, if just given the answer.*

## JOHN 12.1–8

*Six days before the Passover celebration began, Jesus arrived in Bethany, the home of Lazarus— the man he had raised from the dead. ²A dinner was prepared in Jesus' honor. Martha served, and Lazarus was among those who ate with him. ³Then Mary took a twelve-ounce jar of expensive perfume made from essence of nard, and she anointed Jesus' feet with it, wiping his feet with her hair. The house was filled with the fragrance.*

*⁴But Judas Iscariot, the disciple who would soon betray him, said, ⁵"That perfume was worth a year's wages. It should have been sold and the money given to the poor." ⁶Not that he cared for the poor—he was a thief, and since he was in charge of the disciples' money, he often stole some for himself.*

*⁷Jesus replied, "Leave her alone. She did this in preparation for my burial. ⁸You will always have the poor among you, but you will not always have me."*

(SUGGESTED ADDITIONAL READING:
LUKE 10.38–42;
JOHN 1.1–6, 17–20, 28–44)

## NOTES & OBSERVATIONS

Refer to page 8 for guidance on how to dig deeper into the story.

*Where does this take place?*

*When does this take place? See John 12.12.*

***Note:*** *Essence of nard is from the spikenard plant grown in India. Because of the difficulty of transporting this all the way from India, it made this perfume highly expensive. This wasn't just a little one-ounce jar but twelve ounces. A year's wages.*

# REFLECTION

1.  What do you see reflected in Mary's heart by what she gave and how she gave it?

2.  Why do you think the opinions of others did not matter to her?

3.  How did Jesus respond to her?

4.  How is Mary's lavish gift, proof she is living in the wonder of God?

# DAY 2
# GOD'S BIGGER STORY

*As we step into this chapter together, I feel the need to tell you . . . buckle up, we're in for a bumpy ride. This is an uncomfortable one. My heart is squirming even as I write this. Honestly, I don't really want to explore this propensity I have to make God small.*

*You might be inclined to skip over this chapter. But please do not. This is where things get real. It will be hard hitting and disconcerting. But if we are to live dangerously for God, we must pull back the curtain and take a hard look at the real truth.*

*This is where God moves. This is where He shakes us from our habits of mediocrity and walks us into the unexpected. This is where hearts of obedience are formed, and dangerous living begins.*

*Lord, unsettle our hearts for what unsettles Yours. Give us the strength to allow You to walk down into the dungeons of our soul and carry our ugly out into Your glorious light. We know this is where true life is found. It's all because of Jesus, we pray. Amen.*

## Pocket-sized God

I want God . . . just not too much of Him.

I want enough of Him to get what I want. But not enough to make me uncomfortable. I want safe not unpredictable. I want the kind of God I can walk on a leash or carry around in my pocket and who will give me what I think I need. Nothing too out there. And definitely not so big that people will notice. I don't want enough of Him to have to forgive the betrayal of my spouse. Or love a friend who has stabbed me in the back. Or forfeit my plans for His. I want security. A well-defined map. I don't do unknown. I want a God I can control. Someone I understand.

I want God . . . just not too much of Him.

It's hard to admit, but this is where most of us find ourselves. Before you throw up the barriers and think, "Thank God, that's not me", will you consider this?

Have you ever taken control?

Have you ever worried or fretted about something?

Have you ever questioned His character?

Have you ever limited God in any way?

Have you ever said no because it didn't feel safe?

Whether we like it or not, each one of these responses diminishes God's glory and makes Him small.

It's in our nature to want to make Him like us. To expect Him to operate the way we operate. To think the way we think. To be small and manageable. But that's not who God is.

*What attitudes, actions, and thoughts have made God small in your life? How have they made Him small? (Example: Jealousy—You're not giving me what I want. I know better than You.)*

# His Ways Are Not Our Ways

*"My thoughts are nothing like your thoughts,"* says the LORD. *"And my ways are far beyond anything you could imagine"* (Isaiah 55.8).

His ways are far above our ways. We're not even in the same realm. We might know this truth about God, but there's a gap between our head and our heart.

The plain truth is God is beyond our understanding and outside our comprehension.

Take a few minutes to read aloud the following words (don't rush through it) and let God fill you with the AWE of who He is.

*I saw the Lord. He was sitting on a lofty throne, and the train of his robe filled the Temple. Attending him were mighty seraphim,* *each having six wings. With two wings they covered their faces, with two they covered their feet, and with two they flew. They were calling out to each other,*

> *"Holy, holy, holy is the LORD of*
> *Heaven's Armies!*
> *The whole earth is filled with*
> *his glory!"*

*Their voices shook the Temple to its foundations, and the entire building was filled with smoke.*

*Then I said, "It's all over! I am doomed, for I am a sinful man. I have filthy lips, and I live among a people with filthy lips. Yet I have seen the **King**, the LORD of Heaven's Armies.*

*Then one of the seraphim flew to me with a burning coal he had taken from the altar with a pair of tongs. He touched my lips with it and said, "See, this coal has touched your lips. Now your guilt is removed, and your sins are forgiven."*

—Isaiah 6.1–7

Isaiah took one look at God and knew his fate was sealed. He was a dead man.

The mighty AWESOME glory, brilliance, and holiness of God is too much for any human being to survive. And Isaiah knew it. The only chance for salvation had to come from God Himself, and thankfully, He made a way, not just for Isaiah but for us as well.

In this age of political correctness, irreverence, and denial of absolute truth, we have lost the AWE of God. We have resorted to seeing God as our puppet. We pull the strings, and He does what we want. We minimize His holiness, diminish His power, and make Him small.

# *Shapeshifter*

Sin tricks us into thinking we can do a better job than God, so we appoint ourselves as god, in His stead. This is pride. Pride says, "I'm God, and you're not. Pride puts self on the throne as the supreme ruler of our lives.

When we sweep away all the distracting paraphernalia of our sin, at the core we will always see, an underlying desire to be our own god.

It was behind the first sin ever committed. Look at what Satan tells Eve, *"You won't die!" the serpent replied to the woman. "God knows that your eyes will be opened as soon as you eat it, and **you will be like God**, knowing both good and evil"* (Genesis 3.4–5).

A desire to be his own god was behind Satan's rebellion against God.

Satan said, *"**I will** ascend to heaven and set my throne above God's stars. **I will** preside on the mountain of the gods far away in the north. **I will** climb to the highest heavens and **be like the Most High**"* (Isaiah 14.13–14).

This is PRIDE; the innate desire to be god.

It's easy to think, "I'm not really a very a prideful person. I don't boast about my accomplishments. I'm not arrogant. Pride has no hold on me."

Oh really? Could it be that in even thinking this, there is pride?

You see, in the words of my friend Leith Hoggard, "Pride is a shape-shifter."

It comes in all shapes and sizes. Pride cloaks itself in self-abasement, which is easily misunderstood for humility. Pride assumes the shape of serving others but is really seeking the approval of others. Pride appears to surrender and walk in obedience when it is really checking-off-the-list and earning its own way. Pride claims to know all about God yet doesn't really **know** Him. Pride quotes God's promises to others but doesn't live in those promises. Pride justifies its actions and refuses to listen to correction.

Pride masks itself in insecurity. Pride refuses to live in the awe of God and instead makes Him small. **Pride is a shape-shifter.**

If pride is so pervasive and insidious in our lives, the big question is: How do we get rid of it?

The simple but never easy answer is SURRENDER—climbing off our throne and giving Jesus His rightful place in our lives as Supreme Ruler.

## The Hard Work of Surrender

As I have mentioned numerous times, but in case you haven't picked up on it, I'm a control freak. At least now I can say I'm in recovery, however I think it will be a lifetime process. God started this journey of surrender with my relationship with my husband, but He wasn't satisfied with only that area— He began to point out other parts of my life where I was seizing control. The next on the list was my kids.

We had dedicated our kids to the Lord and verbally acknowledged they were His, but it simply was not true. I would occasionally ask God for help, but I had my arms tightly around them. And because I carried the sole responsibility for their care and welfare (another area where I had shut my husband out), I frequently found myself lying awake wracked with fear and worry for the future of my children. After all, it was up

to me and me alone to make sure they didn't turn into axe murderers.

It was another sleepless night of worry. I was face down on my bed, a complete mess. And God and I had a conversation. It went something like this . . .

*"Give them to Me."*

"Isn't that what I did when we dedicated them at church?"

*"Yes, you went through the motions, but did you really give them to Me?"*

Ouch.

"But God, I don't know what it looks like to let them go. How am I supposed to discipline and guide them? How am I supposed to be their mom?"

*"Give them to Me."*

"But God, what if I look like a bad parent. What will people think?"

*"Trust Me, Kristi. Give them to Me."*

I knew I couldn't continue living this way. I was stuck in the crazy-making cycle. Fear was the dictator in our home, and anger, yelling, and taking even more control followed right along in its wake. I was miserable. Our family was in shambles.

It was time to throw in the towel and do it God's way. "Alright, they're Yours. I give them to You. I have no idea what this means or how this will play out, but I'm done. I surrender them to you. They are no longer mine—they are Yours."

The very next day, when one of the kids was naughty, I turned to the Lord and said, "This is your child. What do you want me to do about it?" It was such a simple act, but it made all the difference in the world. As days went by and I continued to follow His guidance and seek His wisdom, I began to realize that I was just the tool He was using to correct and guide *His children*. There was so much freedom. They were no longer my sole responsibility. They were His and it made room for my husband to take over the leadership in our home.

Years later, our oldest son made a series of destructive choices and the old familiar fear and worry began to plague my heart again. But because God and I had done the hard work of rooting this sin out of my life, I was able to acknowledge what this was and step back into the practices I had formed in trusting God with my child.

In my mind, I pictured picking up my son and handing him back to God, saying, "He's not mine, He Yours." Peace (for two seconds). Then the fear and anxiety would overwhelm me, and I would realize he was back in my arms. So I would picture, once again, picking him up (he was way too big to literally pick up) then saying to God, "He's not mine; He's Yours." Over and over again. And as I did this, the space of peace got longer and longer and the worry, shorter and shorter, until I no longer needed to think about doing it. It had become a way of life. This is the hard work of surrender.

SURRENDER makes room for God. **Surrender allows the Holy Spirit to fill our lives with His power and presence.**

## *Holy Spirit Power*

When we open the door to Jesus and welcome Him into our lives, amazing things happen in that moment. We are changed, sealed, baptized, indwelt by the Holy Spirit.

We now have the potential to live a a life of victory over sin and share our faith in the power of the Holy Spirit.[18]

---

18 Bill Bright, *Ten Basic Steps Toward Christian Maturity, Step 3: The Christian & The Holy Spirit* (Peachtree City, GA: Cru, 2003), 1.

We are given this potential, but do we let it become reality in our lives?

Let me illustrate it this way. The wind is a great source of power. When the sails of a boat are aligned to catch the wind, the power of the wind will propel the craft across the water at great speed. But when the sails are not turned so that the wind can fill them, the boat comes to a standstill. Tossed on the waves and dead in the water.

So it is with the Holy Spirit. When we receive Him, we have the potential for victory over sin. We have the potential to live dangerously for the Kingdom, but it isn't until we align our sails to catch "The Wind" and allow Him to fill our lives, that we move and thrive in our spiritual life. This "filling of our sails" by the wind of the Holy Spirit happens when we pitch our paddles overboard and surrender to His power. We give Him control.

In Ephesian 5, Paul challenges the Ephesians when he says, *"Don't be drunk with wine, because that will ruin your life. Instead, be filled with the Holy Spirit."*

Why does Paul compare drunkness to being filled with the Holy Spirit? It seems shocking. When someone is controlled by alcohol how do they behave? They're often out of control, uninhibited, doing things they never would have dreamed of doing in their "right mind".

The Corinthian believers knew very well what someone looked like who was drunk.

I believe Paul used this comparison to help them see clearly what a life would look like when it was filled by the Holy Spirit. This Spirit filling isn't an ethereal intangible goal but a reality every believer can experience. When a follower of Jesus is controlled by the Spirit, they will be bold. Uninhibited. Doing things, they never dreamed possible in their old self.

On the Day of Pentecost, recorded in Acts 2, when the Holy Spirit came upon the apostles, some of the people thought they were drunk. Why? Because they were doing things they would never do in and of themselves. The onlookers knew they were being controlled by something other than themselves and assumed it was alcohol.

So how are we to be filled with the Spirit? How do we let the "Wind" fill our sails? After all that is the command, right?

The answer-again-SURRENDER. When we give up control, we are aligning our sails with the "Wind," and He propels us forward and empowers us to do things we could never do in our own strength.

Jesus said, *"No one can serve two masters"* (Matthew 6.24). If we're in charge, then the Holy Spirit is not.

We must surrender and relinquish our status as supreme ruler. By doing this, we say yes to His way and no to ours. We align our sails with the wind and give the Holy Spirit and His power free reign in our lives. And make no mistake, this power is what raised Jesus from the dead! (see Romans 8.11).

This kind of obedience opens the door to dangerous living because we will find ourselves doing things, we never dreamed we would do. Going places, we never dreamed, we would go. Living lives marked with courage and boldness, not in our own strength and power but in His. Daring to live dangerously for God.

Paul told the Galatians, "*Those who belong to Christ Jesus have nailed the passions and desires of their sinful nature to his cross and crucified them there.* **Since we are living by the Spirit, let us follow the Spirit's leading in every part of our lives**" (Galatians 5.24–25).

## The Surrender Struggle

Confession time. I have this proclivity to nail my passions and desires to the cross only to find myself hightailing it right back to yank them off. I go back to what I know. What's comfortable and safe. Why?

Because, once again, I've appointed myself as supreme ruler of my life. I no longer align my sails with the Wind, instead I fish my paddles out of the water and attempt to live in my own strength.

It's easy to just want a little of God; a friend to wipe away our tears, love us unconditionally, and soften the jagged edges of our lives. It's dreadfully uncomfortable, when He takes a chisel and begins to chip away at us. Or when He calls us out on the end of a limb, and we swear we can hear the faint sound of sawing!

It's easy to diminish God's greatness and glory and try to make Him likes us. But is that really what we want? A God who is lim-

ited and finite. Would this limited and finite god ever have given His Son as a sacrifice for us?

God is so much more than we can understand or fathom. *For the LORD Most High is awesome. He is the great King of all the earth* (Psalm 47.2).

When we remove ourselves as supreme ruler and surrender to God, we unshackle Him from the chains we have held Him in, and we live in wonder of who He is. Our sails are aligned to catch the fresh wind of the Holy Spirit and we live in His power; bold, courageous, and obedient princess warriors.

Will you dare to set Him free in your life and live in the wonder and awe of who He is? Will you surrender to His power and control?

Now is the time to let God be God and dare to live dangerously for His Kingdom.

# DAY 3
# DIG DEEPER INTO THE STORY

## JOHN 15.1–17

"I am the true grapevine, and my Father is the gardener. ²He cuts off every branch of mine that doesn't produce fruit, and he prunes the branches that do bear fruit so they will produce even more. ³You have already been pruned and purified by the message I have given you. ⁴Remain in me, and I will remain in you. For a branch cannot produce fruit if it is severed from the vine, and you cannot be fruitful unless you remain in me.

⁵"Yes, I am the vine; you are the branches. Those who remain in me, and I in them, will produce much fruit. For apart from me you can do nothing. ⁶Anyone who does not remain in me is thrown away like a useless branch and withers. Such branches are gathered into a pile to be burned. ⁷But if you remain in me and my words remain in you, you may ask for anything you want, and it will be granted! ⁸When you produce much fruit, you are my true disciples. This brings great glory to my Father.

⁹"I have loved you even as the Father has loved me. Remain in my love. ¹⁰When you obey my commandments, you remain in my love, just as I obey my Father's commandments and remain in his love. ¹¹I have told you these things so that

## NOTES & OBSERVATIONS

Refer to page 8 for guidance on how to dig deeper into the story.

*Where does this conversation take place?*

*Why might that be significant?*

*you will be filled with my joy. Yes, your joy will overflow!* ¹²*This is my commandment: Love each other in the same way I have loved you.* ¹³*There is no greater love than to lay down one's life for one's friends.* ¹⁴*You are my friends if you do what I command.* ¹⁵*I no longer call you slaves, because a master doesn't confide in his slaves. Now you are my friends, since I have told you everything the Father told me.* ¹⁶*You didn't choose me. I chose you. I appointed you to go and produce lasting fruit, so that the Father will give you whatever you ask for, using my name.* ¹⁷*This is my command: Love each other."*

*Who is the Gardener?*

*Who is the Vine?*

1. What is the job of the:

   Gardener: (v. 2–3)


   Vine (in relationship to the branches): (v. 5)


   Branches: (v. 5,)


2. What is the opposite of remain?




3. What three things are we as the branches to REMAIN in? (v. 5, 7, 9)




4. How do we remain in Christ's love?




5. Can we read our Bible and not remain in His Word? Why or why not? What does someone look like who remains in His Words?

6.   Can we work at a soup kitchen and not remain in His love? Why or Why not? What does someone look like who remains in His love?

7.   Who gets the glory when we, the branches, bear much fruit?

8.   What is the first step you will to take to REMAIN in Christ and live in the WONDER of the Gardener?

# DAY 4
# PAUSE AND REFLECT ON THE STORY

*I will meditate on your majestic, glorious splendor and your wonderful miracles.*
*Your **awe-inspiring** deeds will be on every tongue; I will proclaim your greatness.*
—Psalm 145.5–6

What has God been speaking to you regarding what you have just read and studied in Chapter 6?

What challenged you?

What encouraged you?

*Yours, O Lord, is the greatness, the power, the glory, the victory, and the majesty.*
*Everything in the heavens and on earth is yours, O Lord, and this is Your kingdom.*
*We adore you as the one who is over all things. Wealth and honor come from you alone,*
*for you rule over everything. Power and might are in your hand, and at your discretion*
*people are made great and given strength.*

—1 Chronicles 29.11–12

# Reflecting on the Wonder of God

Here's a simple exercise of prayer that might encourage you to see the greatness and wonder of God in your life. Try thinking of one thing you ADORE about God for each letter of the alphabet. Feel free to take some creative license with challenging letters.

A lmighty

B _____

C _____

D _____

E _____

F _____

G _____

H _____

I _____

J _____

K _____

L _____

M _____

N _____

O _____

P _____

Q _____

R _____

S _____

T _____

U _____

V _____

W _____

X _____

Y _____

Z _____

# DAY 5
# DARE TO LIVE THE STORY
## *Betty*

BETTY JEAN CYPERT WAS BORN IN Washington, Oklahoma in her aunt's bedroom on May 3, 1934. Franklin Delano Roosevelt was president, a loaf of bread cost eight cents and a gallon of gas was ten cents. The whole country was in the middle of the Great Depression.

In the eighty-six years Betty has been alive, she has witnessed incredible changes. As the world went to war against the Nazis, she experienced blackouts and air raid drills. She witnessed the building and tearing down of the Berlin Wall and lived through the Cuban Missile Crisis when the country was on the brink of nuclear war. She mourned, with the rest of her nation, the death of John F. Kennedy and has seen fifteen presidents take office.

Betty listened to the radio and wept when she heard the news of the bombing of Pearl Harbor. She gazed in wonder at her black and white television, when Apollo landed on the moon and heard the famous words by astronaut Neil Armstrong. She was stunned as she watched in horror as the planes hit the World Trade Center.

Betty has not only seen dramatic changes in history, she has seen the world turned upside down with the explosion of technology. Who knew Apples were not just for eating? That people can twitter just as much as birds, and bytes won't hurt you. She discovered that surfing wasn't only for young people anymore, and a yahoo wasn't just a no-good scoundrel trying to steal her money.

However, the greatest cataclysmic event, the one moment when everything changed for her, wasn't when she got an iPad, lived through a war, or even the birth of her first child; it was the day she invited Jesus into her life.

Betty was seventeen years old, when she dared to live in the Wonder of God and promised to follow Him. For months she had been begging Him to come into her life but she didn't really know if He had. She loved Jesus and wanted Him, but she struggled with feeling like a hypocrite. Shame and fear of what others might think kept her from completely letting go. Then a friend invited her to go to a Bible camp, and it was there, while listening to one of the speakers, that she realized she didn't care who knew her failings. She wanted Jesus and Jesus alone. She stood up at the invitation and walked to the front to talk with the pastor. She poured out her heart to him, explaining how unsure she was about whether she was God's child or not. He looked at her and said, "Betty, there's no better time than right now to make sure." And she did.

From that moment on, Betty never looked back . . . she had a surety in heart. She understood she was marked as God's very own daughter. And deep down in her soul, she knew, He had rescued her and set her feet upon the solid rock. She was forever forgiven.

During her teen years Betty devoured books about missionaries, and as she read these amazing stories of God's call on ordinary people to share the Good News around the world, she felt a stirring in her soul to do the same.

God brought a young man into her life who had the same call on his heart as she did, and they were married on December 29, 1961. Just one year later they headed to Alaska to serve as missionaries. Their ministry included administrating and teaching at a Christian boarding school for native Alaskan high school students.

Living fifty miles from the nearest town brought many challenges.

Hardships in this hostile wilderness abounded. Betty and her husband, lived in a Quonset hut with no running water, with a "honey bucket" for evening toilet needs (the bucket was emptied every morning by "honey"), and an outhouse up the hill. Students would drive an old truck to a natural spring, where they would fill large, aluminum milk cans with water and haul to their home.

These were times filled with laughter and tears. Times of incredible beauty and unsettling frustration. Times of joy and times of hardship. Lifelong friendships were forged with fellow missionaries. Three of Betty's four children would be born there. High school students were radically changed by Jesus. Seeing them return to their villages and share God's love and forgiveness with others, even to this day, made all the pain and hardship worthwhile.

They would serve in Alaska for almost ten years before God called them to make a drastic move to California. There they would continue their ministry to young people, as her husband took a position as dean of a Bible institute in the Sacramento area. Their passion and mission to which God called them has always been and continues to be, "discipling others who will go and make disciples." After eight years of ministry at the Bible school, they moved to Southern California and switched vocations.

Pastoring a small church brought many challenges and much heartache.

It would've been easy for Betty to let her heart grow hard toward God and His people, but she refused to let that happen. This soft heart allowed God to mold and shape her into the woman He desired her to be. The lessons she learned during this heartbreaking time were invaluable. And God was so faithful. He restored the years of hurt and gave them ten beautiful years with a new church family who loved them dearly and brought healing to their wounded hearts.

In later years, they would serve as missionaries, once again, in Lawrenceville, Georgia. Before Zoom was even a thought, you could find her meeting regularly with a young Chinese woman she had met in a restaurant while they Skyped with her friend in China. And their home would often have young people gathering for a time of worship and encouragement, all while enjoying the homemade cookies she had made.

Betty has followed Jesus for sixty-nine years. A lifetime of loving Him. The greatest gift Betty has carried with her into these later years is this: Her sin was paid in full by the death of her Savior. He died so she might LIVE, and she is doing just that.

This lady, beautiful both inside and out, is my mother. And as her child, I can honestly say she didn't just talk the talk, she walked it. I knew from an early age that Jesus was everything to her. On rare occasions, I would wake up early, before the sun had risen. I would tiptoe my way out to the living room and see her sitting in her favorite chair, Bible open on her lap, spending time with the Lord she loved. Her life, the way she lived and loved, has shaped me into the woman I am today.

Betty is on the doorstep of heaven. Her body is slowly fading away. She spends most of her days in a chair by her window. It hurts deep down to see this woman, once so full of life, slowed down because of her failing body. But it hasn't changed her love and passion for her Savior. Last year, even though it was difficult for her to read and focus, she worked her way through the entire Bible.

Sitting with her recently, I asked her, "Mom, what does Jesus mean to you?" She sat back in her chair, lifted her head and gazed upward, "Jesus is EVERYTHING to me. He is all I need."

In response I pulled out my iPhone and played a song she loves, "King Forevermore," written by Mom's friend Aaron Keyes and Pete James. There was no special lighting, no words on the screen, no live band playing, just mom and me and an iPhone, but it was one of the most beautiful moments of worship I have ever experienced. The tears poured down my cheeks as I watched my precious mother in her blue recliner, hands, eyes, and heart lifted toward heaven. Mouthing the words because she can no longer use her beautiful voice. Singing praise to the ONE who is everything to her.

*God, the Uncreated One*
*The Author of Salvation*
*Wrote the laws of space and time*
*And fashioned worlds to His design*
*The One whom angel hosts revere*
*Hung the stars like chandeliers*
*Numbered every grain of sand*
*Knows the heart of every man*
*He is King forevermore.*

—Aaron Keyes and Pete James[19]

Betty has spent a lifetime allowing God to be BIG in her life. He is her King.

She would be the first to tell you that her walk has not been perfect. In fact, when I told her I wanted to include her story in my book, she said, "Now don't you lie about me!" Worried I might make her sound better than she was. Betty is just an ordinary woman choosing to follow Jesus in the best way she knows how. She continually struggles with selfishness and pride, but she knows she has a Savior who willingly went to the cross to pay the debt she owed. Betty refuses to give in to doubts and fears and instead chooses to live in the wonder of God every day, even as she sits in her blue recliner.

The lives she has touched and the impact she's made for God's Kingdom are like the ripples on a lake after a rock is tossed in; the ripples will continue to be felt long after she is gone. Betty has left an indelible mark on so many, not because of who she is, but because of what she allowed God to do in her and through her. And I am one of them.

Jesus is walking her home and she can't wait to see Him face-to-face. Because long ago, she dared to let God be BIG in her life, and she has continued to make that choice every day since. He is all she needs. He is her everything.

*On August 7, 2020, Betty took her last breath here and her first breath in heaven. I was able to read this book to her just a month before she died. I'm so grateful God gave us that time together. At times, it's hard to believe she is really gone. It takes my breath away when I realize she is no longer able to receive my texts and listen as I share my struggles and joys. But then I'm reminded of where she is and what she is experiencing. I know my sweet mama is sitting at the feet of the Savior she loves and lifting her voice with myriad other voices in praise to her King.*

---

19 *King Forevermore*, 2016, 10000 Fathers, Aaron Keyes and Pete James. Used by permission

# What About Us?

What is keeping you from living in the wonder of God?

Fear? Disillusionment? Pride? Need for control? Doubt? Something else?

Confess your sin before God. You're already forgiven, this just makes things right between you and God and removes the blockage, so the Holy Spirit has the freedom to work in your life. Next, dare to confess your struggles to a friend, one you know will pray for you, not judge you but will speak truth to you.

James tells us, *"Confess your sins to each other and pray for each other so that you may be healed.* ***The earnest prayer of a righteous person has great power and produces wonderful results"*** (James 5.16).

I have found this promise to be true in my own life. Remember my friend Lisa, the prayer warrior? One day I told her I was struggling and back in the stronghold that had held me captive for so long. I confessed how I had lost sight of what God had done for me and had crawled back into my comfortable place. I asked her to pray for me.

The next day she sent me a picture of a chapter she was reading in a book. She was so excited because it was specifically talking about strongholds. (God is amazing like that!) The part she had highlighted stated that the best way to loosen the ties of your stronghold was to fast and pray. As I read those words my heart sank. I hate fasting. Probably because it's connected to my stronghold—food. As I read the text she sent me, I thought, *Lord, I just can't do it. I've fasted and prayed once a week for eight months and I just can't do it again. I don't have it in me.*

So, I texted her back a generic "Thanks," and left it at that.

But she didn't stop there, she sent another text, "God has pressed it upon my heart to fast and pray for you today." Reading that simple text opened the floodgate, as I experienced the love of a friend willing to make this sacrifice for me, even though I was completely unwilling to do it. God used the faithful prayer of a righteous woman to accomplish so much in my life!

Confessing to a friend is humbling. We would much rather present a victorious front instead of a defeated one. But it is in the vulnerability, in the refusal to keep things hidden away, and the willingness to bring our sins out into the Light, where God does His greatest work in us.

# My prayer for you

I pray that _____, will understand the **incredible greatness of**
*(insert your name)*

**God's power** when she believes Him. **This is the same mighty power that raised Christch from the dead** and seated him in the place of honor at God's right hand in the heavenly realms.

(Prayer based on Ephesians 1.19–20)

# Will you dare to live dangerously and live in the wonder of God?

*Week 7*

# DARE TO EMBRACE THE MESSY MIDDLE

*God's grace meets us in messy places because messy places are all that there are.*

— TULLIAN TCHIVIDJIAN[20]

Jesus, our hearts yearn for you. We are weary of living on this planet with all its sin and brokenness. We are tired of this yo-yo dance between Your Kingdom and ours. We long for the day when we will see You face-to face-and experience our real true HOME. But for now, this is where You have us. So, teach us how to embrace the uncomfortable. Show us how to live in this messy-middle space. Give us eyes to see beyond our circumstances to Your Kingdom work. May we know Your infinite grace and power for whatever comes our way. Amen.

---

20 Tullian Tchividjian, Facebook post February 14, 2016.

# DAY 1
# AN ANCIENT STORY
## *Jochebed*

SHE FELT LIKE AN ANVIL WAS SITTING ON HER chest. She could barely breathe. How could they have let this happen? What would her husband, Amram, say? *We were so incredibly foolish.* A moment of passion and a lifetime of regret. *It shouldn't be this way. We are husband and wife after all.*

She had noticed her cycle had not come for a couple of months but had attributed it to stress. But now she knew for sure, it wasn't.

This morning, she had luxuriated in a few stolen moments of quiet and peace before her day began. Amram had risen early for his day of labor as a slave. And then she had felt it. *No, it can't be. It's probably just gas.* No! There it was again.

She knew all too well the familiar feeling of this little bird in her belly. She put her hand on the spot, and all doubt was removed.

She should be happy. They should be happy. They had wanted more children. But not now. Everything had changed.

She was with her dear friend Miriam (the woman they named their daughter after), when the soldiers came and ripped her pre-cious newborn baby boy from her arms. The echoes of her wailing still haunted her.

Their whole community was in pain. There was so much heartbreak everywhere it felt as if even the walls were crying.

This was the stuff of nightmares.

And now this was her nightmare. *Maybe I will have a girl . . . than all will be well. But what if this baby is a boy?* She couldn't even think about it.

Amram and Jochebed had only ever known slavery. Their parents were slaves and their grandparents before them. For four hundred years, their people had been slaves in this foreign land of Egypt.

Long, long ago their ancestor Abraham had come seeking refuge from the raging famine. Joseph, his son, was Prime Minister at the time, and clearly God had positioned him so that he might rescue Abraham and his family.

But that had been centuries before and now the cruel Egyptians were fearful of how vast in number the Israelites had become. So the Egyptians made living hard. Back break-ing work was made even harder by unreason-able demands. And to control their numbers,

Pharaoh had recently ordered every baby boy to be killed.

Amram and Jochebed already had two children: Miriam and Aaron. Because of Pharaoh's decree they had chosen not to have any more.

*That was their plan but evidently God had a different one.*

As she watched her belly grow bigger every month, Jochebed's heart felt like it was being torn in two. She was so excited to hold this little one to her breast. To count her fingers and toes. To smell the sweet scent of her newborn child. *It just has to be a girl.*

*But what if it is a boy?* She could feel the noose of fear tighten around her throat as it threatened to choke the life out of her. How could she go on? *What are we going to do?*

She remained hidden away from anyone who might report her pregnancy, when all she wanted was to announce to the world the coming of this precious addition to their family. Why did it have to be this way? What hope was there for this little one; it was either slavery or death.

She bit down on the wooden slat the midwife gave her, to keep from yelling out. Oh the pain! *How could I have forgotten how painful becoming a mother is?* She had to keep quiet. But how could she?

Time blurred, minutes turned into hours and hours into days. It felt like an eternity. But finally, it was time to push. Time to welcome this little one into this mess of a world

they were in. Bearing down she felt the release as the tiny body slid out and away from her.

Her heart was filled with hope that it was a girl. But as the midwife held him up, Jochebed's heart sank.

*What will we do? How can we save this little one from the cruel hand of Pharaoh?*

Jochebed pulled her precious boy close to her chest and wondered about his future. Her hungry eyes searched every beautiful part of him. She couldn't get enough of this amazing creature laying in her arms. There was something different about him. He was special. Even her husband Amram saw the difference.

Gazing at this sweet gift, she knew she had to do whatever it took to protect his life.

They were able to hide him for three months, but now his cries were louder and the soldiers more vigilant in their quest for Israelite baby boys. They had to do something and do it quickly, if they were to save their son.

Jochebed had seen Pharaoh's daughter bathe in the Nile with her servant girls surrounding her. She'd observed the lack of guards and knew that if anyone would be drawn to caring for an "abandoned" child she would.

A river of tears soaked the reedy basket, as she stowed her tiny son inside. She had spent days first making the basket then tarring and pitching it, so it would keep her tiny boy safe and dry.

Before she placed him in his little "nest," she held him close and watched his tiny mouth suckle her breast one last time. How could a mother give up her son to a stranger? How could she do this? *But what choice do I have? I have to save my precious child.*

She hid him in the reeds of the Nile River, near the place where she knew the princess would come to bathe, and left Miriam to watch over the basket.

The hours seemed to drag by as questions plagued her mind. *What if she doesn't come? What if she orders him to be killed? What if a crocodile or a soldier finds him first? What if there was a better way to save him?* The tormenting questions assaulted her as she paced back and forth in her tiny home.

And then finally Miriam was there, out of breath and talking a mile a minute. "Mother, she wants you to come right now. I told her that I knew of someone who could feed and care for the baby and she wants to meet you. She'll even pay you to care for him."

Hope filled her heart as she ran to meet Pharaoh's daughter. Time stood still as she watched the princess place her very own child in her arms and ask her to take care of him.

God had saved her son. He had heard her prayers. And He continued to give her blessing upon blessing as she nurtured and cared for her son in the formative years of his little life.

She knew the day would come when she would have to give him back. It would be the hardest thing she would ever do. How she would do it, she had no idea. But she was convinced God would give her the strength when the time came.

This little boy was born for something special, this she knew. He wasn't hers; he was God's.

One day, her arms would be empty, she would still be in slavery, and life would be a new normal. But she had learned she could trust in the God of her ancestor Abraham. God had miraculously rescued her son, and she knew He would rescue them, too.

# Taking a Deeper Look

*In this section, it is your turn to take a deeper look at this story in God's Word and see for yourself the truth that lies within. These questions are intended to be a guide as you search for the treasure. If you don't know the answers to some of the questions, it's okay. Not knowing all the answers is not a bad thing. My hope is that it will cause you to think more deeply and explore Scripture in ways you might never have, if just given the answer.*

## EXODUS 2.1-10

*About this time, a man and woman from the tribe of Levi got married. ²The woman became pregnant and gave birth to a son. She saw that he was a special baby and kept him hidden for three months. ³But when she could no longer hide him, she got a basket made of papyrus reeds and waterproofed it with tar and pitch. She put the baby in the basket and laid it among the reeds along the bank of the Nile River. ⁴The baby's sister then stood at a distance, watching to see what would happen to him.*

*⁵Soon Pharaoh's daughter came down to bathe in the river, and her attendants walked along the riverbank. When the princess saw the basket among the reeds, she sent her maid to get it for her. ⁶When the princess opened it, she saw the baby. The little boy was crying, and she felt sorry for him. "This must be one of the Hebrew children," she said.*

*⁷Then the baby's sister approached the princess. "Should I go and find one of the Hebrew women to nurse the baby for you?" she asked.*

## NOTES & OBSERVATIONS

Refer to page 8 for guidance on how to dig deeper into the story.

*Describe the "messy middle" Jochebed is in? (Messy middle is defined as the center of a difficult or challenging experience that is out of a someone's control.)*

*8"Yes, do!" the princess replied. So the girl went and called the baby's mother.*

*9"Take this baby and nurse him for me," the princess told the baby's mother. "I will pay you for your help." So the woman took her baby home and nursed him.*

*10Later, when the boy was older, his mother brought him back to Pharaoh's daughter, who adopted him as her own son. The princess named him Moses, for she explained, "I lifted him out of the water."*

ADDITIONAL SUGGESTED READING:
EXODUS 1

**Note:** Jochebed and the nation of Isreal have been in captivity for four hundred years. The last time anyone has had any word from God was with Joseph and Abraham. Their only knowledge and understanding about God has come from what has been passed down through generations. Yet we see an amazing, resolute faith in the heart of Jochebed. This is a miracle and a testimony to the power of God.

# REFLECTION

*It was by faith that Moses' parents hid him for three months when he was born. They saw that God had given them an unusual child, and they were not afraid to disobey the king's command.*

—HEBREWS 11.23

1.  How did Jochebed prove her faith was in God?

2.  What core belief in God did these parents have that gave them the courage to defy Pharaoh's command? Explain.

3.  Does courage negate fear? Why or why not?

In Exodus 6.20 and Numbers 26.59, we see Jochebed's name. Besides what is written in Hebrews, there is no other mention of Jochebed than these verses from Exodus 2. We have no idea whether she watches her son, Moses, lead her people into freedom. From all accounts, it is very possible she died, never tasting freedom, never experiencing the leadership of Moses. Both of Moses's siblings, Aaron and Miriam, play key roles in the future of Israel, and even Moses's father-in-law is mentioned but not his parents. Jochebed most likely was in this "messy middle" her whole life.

4.  Do you believe God is still good when He leaves people in their messy middles? Why or why not?

5.  What do you learn about God in this story?

# DAY 2
# GOD'S BIGGER STORY

*There's something that's not right or not perfect or not the way we had hoped or dreamed that it was going to be. But God promises He will use everything and every moment to ultimately take us to a new Heaven and a new Earth. For now, we're stuck in the middle.*

—Louie Giglio

## Stuck in the Middle

The middle—neither here nor there but somewhere in between.

Life is full of middles . . .

- Middle kids. The ones with the least amount of pictures and most likely to be left somewhere.

- Midlife crisis. Unhappy where we've been and dissatisfied with where we're going.

- Middle airplane seats. Enough said.

The middle is often uncomfortable, unsettling, and messy.

But did you know, this is where followers of Jesus live? In the messy middle. Pulled between two realms. Living in this world but belonging to the next.

Here's how Paul described messy-middle living.

*For instance, we know that when these bodies of ours are taken down like tents and folded away, they will be replaced by resurrection bodies in heaven—God-made, not handmade—and we'll never have to relocate our "tents" again.* **Sometimes we can hardly wait to move—and so we cry out in frustration. Compared to what's coming, living conditions around here seem like a stopover in an unfurnished shack, and we're tired of it!** *We've been given a glimpse of the real thing, our true home, our resurrection bodies! The Spirit of God whets our appetite by giving us a taste of what's ahead. He puts a little of heaven in our hearts so that we'll never settle for less.*

—2 Corinthians 5.1–5, MSG

This world is not our home. The problem comes when we forget this. When we expect comfort and safety instead of discomfort and unsettledness. When we pitch our tent and make it our permanent home.

Make no mistake . . . we are in the messy middle; caught between this world and the next. This is not our home.

# Where Is Our Home?

"Welcome home!" the immigration officer said as he checked over my passport.

I wondered . . . Are there any two more beautiful words?

I had just spent a fabulous eleven days in South Korea with my husband and son. For a short time, we had adopted Korean ways. We became chopstick aficionados, sitting on the floor to eat, enjoying pepper paste and kimchi. We lived in a Korean home and took in all the sights, smells, and sounds of South Korea. As incredible as that time was, it didn't change the fact that we were visitors in a foreign land. I felt like a giant and stuck out like a sore thumb with my white skin and red hair. Their language was so foreign, there was nothing to compare it to. No occasional words I could pick up because of their similarity to English. I was awkward in their culture, wondering all the time if I was offending them with my crazy American ways.

We were just travelers passing through, taking in all we could for a few short moments. Then we kissed our son goodbye and stepped back into our old familiar comfortable world.

After a fourteen-hour plane flight, we were finally home. I felt like Dorothy in the Wizard of Oz . . . "There's no place like home. There's no place like home." It was like putting on an old comfy sweater or a favorite pair of worn-out jeans. We were back to where we belonged. Where we could be completely us. Where we were comfortable, and things were familiar. We could read signs, understand what was being said and communicate once again. We. Were. Home.

But is this really my home? Is it your home?

No. This is just a stopping ground, a place to pitch our tents while we await our heavenly lodgings.

There are times when we feel this "outlanderness" more than others. When we talk about God, and people stare at us as if we're speaking a foreign language. When we feel out of place and just don't seem to fit in. When we have a longing deep in our soul for something more. When we struggle in our time alone with God and wish we could see Him face-to-face.

We're reminded this is not our real home.

# Comfort at All Cost

But often, our tendency is to forget. We fail to remember we're travelers, just passing through on our way to our eternal digs. This forgetting causes us to live as though this is all there is. It drives us to put all our dreams and hopes in the basket of this world. The absentmindedness lulls us into hanging the pictures on the wall and settling in.

The apostle Peter speaks about this residency issue in 1 Peter 2.11. (I love how the Message puts it): *"Friends, this world is not your home, so don't make yourselves cozy in it."*

Oh but I love cozy! I crave comfort and cling to the security of the familiar.

What I supremely dislike—Unpredictable. Insecure. Uncomfortable.

*Don't I deserve a well-ordered, well-planned life?*

I hate to admit it but there is this tendency in me to pursue comfort above all.

I don't think I'm the only one.

"Quick, easy, and comfortable" that's the American way. Microwave ovens, Keurig coffee makers, automatic car starters (which I wish I had every time I step out my door in the frozen tundra of Michigan), dishwashers. and the list goes on and on.

During our time in South Korea, my love for comfort stood in stark contrast to all things Korean. The Korean couple we stayed with were so sweet to give us their bedroom. But their bed was rock hard. I'm not kidding. It literally had no give. I even pulled up the covers to see if it was a real mattress or not. Then we discovered from our South Korean daughter-in-love, IT ACTUALLY WAS A ROCK. Marble to be more exact. (Koreans believe it is good for their posture and health.) And along with the marble bed came sand pillows.

In their living room they had a wooden couch and two wooden chairs. For dinner they brought out a small table and we sat on the floor to eat. It had been years since I had sat cross-legged on the floor. It wasn't pretty.

Seriously, I couldn't wait to get home. I dreamed of curling up on my comfortable couch, crawling into my soft bed and snuggling up with my fluffy pillow.

When we returned home, I sank onto my comfy couch and thought, "Oh, I just love comfort." And immediately, I heard God's quiet whisper, "Yes, you do, Kristi, and it has made you a comfortable follower." Ouch!

**I had told God I would follow Him at any cost, but my choices were saying something completely different.** The way I was living said, "I will follow you God if it doesn't cost me too much. If you don't ask me to step out of my comfort zone. If it's safe. If it's what I know I'm good at. If I can be in control. And seriously, don't ask me to love those who are hard to love, or let go of my anger, or surrender my self-righteousness, or make time for You. If I follow You, I expect You to bless me and give me what I want."

# Uncomfortable Following

Nowhere does Jesus promote this idea of comfort at all cost. In fact, it is just the opposite!

Someone said to Jesus, *"I will follow you wherever you go."*

But Jesus replied, *"Foxes have dens to live in, and birds have nests, but the Son of Man has no place even to lay His head"* (Luke 9.57–58).

*"If any of you wants to be my follower, you must give up your own way, take up your cross, and follow Me. If you try to hang on to your life, you will lose it. But if you give up your life for My sake, you will save it"* (Matthew 16.24–25).

*"If you want to be My disciple, you must, by comparison, hate everyone else—your father and mother, wife and children, brothers and sisters—yes, even your own life. Otherwise, you cannot be My disciple"* (Luke 14.26).

Tough words to swallow, in this comfort-loving world we live in.

But the pursuit of comfort will always be contrary to following Jesus. We can't pursue comfort and follow Jesus—it just doesn't work. **Jesus calls us to a life of risk, a life that is foolish in the eyes of the world.** And it is anything but comfortable.

# Messier-Middles

If you're a follower of Jesus, **you are in the messy middle**. Caught between this world and the next, living in a foreign land.

**It is in our messier middles that God pushes us out of the comfortable and into the uncomfortable.** These messier middles slap us in the face and wake us up to the fact that this is not our home . . .

When our husband has lost his job and the bills are stacking up.

When our mother-in-law says one too many cruel things.

When our spouse decides they love someone else.

When our teenager is caught selling dope.

When racism raises its ugly head.

When our arms ache to hold a baby.

When our dreams don't come true.

When our spirits are crushed from a broken friendship or loved one lost.

We aren't home yet. This is the messier middle we ALL are experiencing.

While driving my car one day, I caught the tail end of a radio interview. I never learned the name of the young man being interviewed, but what he said rocked my world.

This young man, in his early twenties had been a drug addict and contracted AIDS. It was after getting AIDS that he came to know Christ as his own personal Savior. The interviewer asked him if he ever questioned why God had allowed such a horrible thing to happen to him. He was so young and had his whole life ahead of him but instead he was dying. (I learned some years later that he died just months after this interview).

The young man in reply to this question said, "Yes, I ask God why all the time!"

**"Why out of all the people in the world, did You choose me? Because now I will spend eternity with You!"**

# Eternity Is Coming

This young man was overwhelmed by God's goodness. He got it. His life here on earth was one simple breath (Psalm 39.5). A short span of time. And yet God had chosen to intersect his brief life and change its course for all ETERNITY.

He was choosing to live life to the full in the messy middle. This wasn't his home. Some people would think it was a tragic end to such a short life. But he knew differently. He knew this wasn't the end. It was just the BEGINNING.

Maybe you need reminding—**God is in your messier middle.** It's His design. This is where He is doing His best work in you. Preparing you for your true home. Eternity isn't the end of your journey. It is just the BEGINNING.

**Where will Home be for You?**

One day Jesus was talking to His disciples. He wanted them to know what the Kingdom of God would be like. So He told a story about a man who was setting out on a long journey. Before he left, he called his three servants together and entrusted them with his money. The first servant received five bags of gold. The second, two bags of gold, and the third, one bag.

The first servant went immediately, put his money to work and gained five more bags. The second servant did the same and gained two more bags. But the third dug a hole and put the bag of gold there for safe keeping.

When the man returned from his journey, he asked each servant to give a report of what they did with the money. As he listened to the first two servants and what they had done with his money, he was ecstatic and exclaimed, *"Well done, good and faithful servant! You have been faithful with a few things; I will put you in charge of many things.*

*Come and share your master's happiness"* (Matthew 25.23 NIV).

But when he heard what the third one had done with his money, he shouted, "You lazy and worthless servant."

Then he gave the money to the first one and ordered the worthless servant to be thrown outside, into the darkness (Matthew 25.14–30).

The first two men chose to risk everything to gain more but the third man played it safe, choosing comfort and security. And what did the master see? A servant who was lazy and worthless.

## Dangerous Living

When we refuse to embrace this messy middle living and choose comfort instead, we are like this last servant, burying our treasure and living safe. But this is not what Jesus died for. This is not how He calls His followers to live.

"Jesus didn't die on the cross to make us safe. Jesus died to make us dangerous."[21]

Jesus is looking for followers who will ruthlessly eliminate the pursuit of comfort from their life and choose risky, dangerous living.

**Friends, this world is not our home. Let's stop living like it is.** Let's stop "living as if the purpose of life is to arrive safely at death."[22]

The Bible tells us, *"No eye has seen, no ear has heard, and no mind has imagined what God has prepared for those who love him"* (1 Corinthians 2.9). Do you believe this?

Do you really believe this? Not just know this truth in your head but are you living this perspective out in your life?

## Not Home Yet

We are not home yet. We are nomads in a foreign land. But one day we will move into our permanent home. One day we will see our Savior face-to-face. One day this world with all its pain and heartache will be gone. One day we will leave this messy-middle living and finally be HOME.

---

21 Mark Batterson, *Wild Goose Chase* (Colorado Springs: Multnomah Books, 2008), 6.
22 Mark Batterson, *Primal: The Lost Soul of Christianity* (Colorado Springs, Multnomah Books, 2009) 150.

*And I saw the holy city, the new Jerusalem, coming down from God out of heaven like a bride beautifully dressed for her husband. I heard a loud shout from the throne, saying,* **"Look, God's home is now among his people! He will live with them, and they will be his people. God Himself will be with them. He will wipe every tear from their eyes, and there will be no more death or sorrow or crying or pain. All these things are gone forever."**

*And the one sitting on the throne said, "Look, I am making everything new!" And then he said to me, "Write this down, for what I tell you is trustworthy and true."*

—REVELATION 21.2–5

But we are not home yet.

We're in the messy middle. This is where God has us. This is where He is shaping and forming us as His children.

Jesus is looking for followers who will EMBRACE the messy middle. They aren't waiting around for things to get less messy. No, instead they throw open wide the doors to this messy middle living because they know this is where He is doing His greatest work in them. This is where His masterpiece begins to take shape, where the once ugly hunk of rock is chiseled and shaped into a beautiful work of art.

*Describe the messy middle you are in right now.*

*What would it look like for you to embrace what God is doing in your messy middle?*

As Jesus followers, **we EMBRACE the messy middle; when we dare to quit trying to fix the mess and welcome the work God is doing in our lives through the mess.** We welcome His work when we dare to give the pursuit of comfort the boot and live dangerously for Him. When we continually live with our eternal perspective in view.

This is our confident hope . . . if you are a true follower of Jesus, one day you will close your eyes here and open them in heaven. And your Savior will be there to greet you with the sweetest words ever spoken, "Welcome HOME!"

This isn't just wishful thinking; it is a guarantee we can count on. It is a promise to hold on to.

For now, we are in the engagement period, stuck in the messy middle.

Friends, our wedding day is coming! Our Groom is preparing our home. Let's dare to **EMBRACE** this messy middle living, so that on our wedding day we will step into heaven with no regrets!

# DAY 3
# DIG DEEPER INTO THE STORY

## 2 CORINTHIANS 5.1-9

*For we know that when this earthly tent we live in is taken down (that is, when we die and leave this earthly body), we will have a house in heaven, an eternal body made for us by God himself and not by human hands. ²We grow weary in our present bodies, and we long to put on our heavenly bodies like new clothing. ³For we will put on heavenly bodies; we will not be spirits without bodies. ⁴While we live in these earthly bodies, we groan and sigh, but it's not that we want to die and get rid of these bodies that clothe us. Rather, we want to put on our new bodies so that these dying bodies will be swallowed up by life. ⁵God himself has prepared us for this, and as a guarantee he has given us his Holy Spirit.*

*⁶So we are always confident, even though we know that as long as we live in these bodies we are not at home with the Lord. ⁷For we live by believing and not by seeing. ⁸Yes, we are fully confident, and we would rather be away from these earthly bodies, for then we will be at home with the Lord. ⁹So whether we are here in this body or away from this body, our goal is to please him.*

## NOTES & OBSERVATIONS

Refer to page 8 for guidance on how to dig deeper into the story.

*What is difficult about your earthly tent living?*

1. How is God preparing you for your eternal home? (v.5)

2. Why is it important for Paul's readers to know that the Holy Spirit is their guarantee? Why is it important for you to know?

   For a more indepth study of the Holy Spirit and His role in our lives, check out these verses: John 14.25, Romans 5.5, Romans 8.11,15, 26, 1 Corinathians 6.19, 2 Corinthians 1.22.

3. What would it look like for you to live "by believing and not by seeing", right now in your present circumstances? (v. 7)

4. What are the reasons, we as believers are "always confident even though we are not home with the Lord yet" (vs. 6)? (see vv. 1–5)

5. Are you living in confidence or doubt?

   a. If you're living in confidence, how does your life show it?

   b. If you're not, what's holding you back?

*"Do we eagerly long for the coming of Christ? Or do we want him to wait while our love affair with the world runs its course? That is the question that tests the authenticity of our faith."*

—John Piper[23]

\* \* \*

One summer, the small group my husband and I were a part of decided it would be fun to go on a camping trip together. For my husband and I, camping with four small boys was about as appealing as having a root canal. But we decided we needed to be "good" group members and participate.

Let me just say, that tenting weekend turned out to be one of the worst weekends of my life. It wasn't the company, it was the tenting. Have you ever been in a tent with four little boys? There's the cooking over an open fire, THE DIRT, the clean up with no running water, THE DIRT, the humidity, the communal toilets, THE DIRT . . .

Then there was the sleeping or the lack of it.

My husband and I were smart (or so we thought)—we brought an air mattress, so we didn't have to lie on the ground but what we didn't bring was an extra blanket to put on top of the air mattress to keep the cold night air from seeping through. I lay awake most of the night dreaming of my soft, warm bed.

My thoughts went something like this: "We are crazy! Our nice warm, comfy, dry, bed is forty-five minutes from here, where there is electricity, running water, flushing toilets, and no DIRT."

When it comes to spiritual tenting, I think I feel the same way I do about physical tenting. I don't like living in a tent! I long for my real home. The home where Jesus is, where I can get a cup of coffee with Him and have a face-to-face conversation. Where there is no more sorrow and no more tears. Where the pain of this life is a distant memory. Where I will have the answers to all my questions. Where I'll see loved ones who've gone on before me. Where there is peace and **no more messiness**.

But I often fail to recognize this longing in my heart and mistake it for something else. Which leads to distraction over this temporary "tent"? I decorate it, fix it up and try to disguise it so that it won't look and feel too much like a tent and yet nothing really changes. I wonder how much time I've wasted focusing on the temporal instead of the eternal.

---

23 John Piper, "Loving the Second Coming and the Assurance of Salvation" (February 11, 1997 Article) Desiring God Foundation, www.desiringGod.org.

Are you settling for less? Have you spent so much time focusing on your "tent" that you have lost sight of your real home? Let God whet your appetite with a taste of what's ahead and never, never, never settle for anything less!

# DAY 4
# PAUSE AND REFLECT ON THE STORY

*Has the Lord rejected me forever? Will he never again be kind to me?*
*Is his unfailing love gone forever? Have his promises permanently failed?*
*Has God forgotten to be gracious? Has he slammed the door on his compassion?*
*And I said, "This is my fate; the Most High has turned his hand against me."*
*But then I recall all you have done, O Lord; I remember your wonderful deeds of long ago.*
*They are constantly in my thoughts. I cannot stop thinking about your mighty works.*
—PSALM 77.7–12

What has God been speaking to you regarding what you have just read and studied in Chapter 7?

What challenged you?

What encouraged you?

**Read aloud the following printed verses.** After reading each translation, copy down the translation that most resonates with you. Make it personal by inserting your name and personal pronouns. As you write, tell God you are listening and ask Him to speak to you through His Word.

## COLOSSIANS 3.1–4, NLT

*Since you have been raised to new life with Christ, set your sights on the realities of heaven, where Christ sits in the place of honor at God's right hand. Think about the things of heaven, not the things of earth. For you died to this life, and your real life is hidden with Christ in God. And when Christ, who is your life, is revealed to the whole world, you will share in all his glory.*

## COLOSSIANS 3.1–4, NIV

*Since, then, you have been raised with Christ, set your hearts on things above, where Christ is, seated at the right hand of God. Set your minds on things above, not on earthly things. For you died, and your life is now hidden with Christ in God. When Christ, who is your life, appears, then you also will appear with him in glory.*

## COLOSSIANS 3.1–4, MSG

*So if you're serious about living this new resurrection life with Christ, act like it. Pursue the things over which Christ presides. Don't shuffle along, eyes to the ground, absorbed with the things right in front of you. Look up, and be alert to what is going on around Christ—that's where the action is. See things from his perspective. Your old life is dead. Your new life, which is your real life—even though invisible to spectators—is with Christ in God. He is your life. When Christ (your real life, remember) shows up again on this earth, you'll show up, too—the real you, the glorious you. Meanwhile, be content with obscurity, like Christ.*

Write out a prayer to God.

# DAY 5
# DARE TO LIVE THE STORY
## *Keri*

Keri is one of those rare people when you meet her for the first time you feel like you've known her your whole life. She has the unique gift of making you feel like you're the most amazing friend she's ever had. I thank God often for bringing her into my life.

Keri and I became friends when she was in the midst of a very messier middle. And honestly, it feels like she's been in one really messy middle after another since I've known her. If there's anyone who doesn't need to be reminded that she's in messy middle living, it's Keri. She has experienced more heartache and brokenness in these few short years, since I've known her, than many people will experience in a lifetime.

Most people, if they were in Keri's shoes, would have given up on God and everybody else a long time ago. They would've thrown in the towel and been done. But not Keri.

In fact, I've watched just the opposite happen. Her heart seems to grow softer with each new difficulty. Her faith unwavering. Her passion to know God and follow Him, unstoppable.

I met Keri and her husband Will as they were getting ready to welcome their new daughter into their family. Their only child, Mayla, would finally be a big sister. But just months into the pregnancy, they received devastating news from the doctor. "Your baby has anencephaly." (Anencephaly is a birth defect where a baby is born without parts of the brain and skull.)

It felt as if her doctor had thrown her in the deep end of the pool and she had forgotten how to swim. She could hear his muffled words, but she couldn't understand them. All she knew was that she was drowning as the diagnosis ripped away all her hopes and dreams for this new little addition to their family,

The next few precious months were bittersweet. A mixture of joy and sorrow. Keri treasured the times of feeling their little sweet Arabella kick and move in her belly, safe and secure in her mama's womb. But she knew all too soon the time would come when Arabella would leave this safe place and be thrust into the world where she would be unable to survive. It felt like her heart would tear in two. How could she walk this difficult road?

But Keri had allowed God to build a strong foundation in her life. She had given her whole heart to Him and experienced His cleansing work in her life. What the prophet Ezekiel says God will do for His nation of Israel is what God did in Keri's life.

*I will give you a new heart, and I will put a new spirit in you. I will take out your stony, stubborn heart and give you a tender, responsive heart. And I will put my Spirit in you so that you will follow my decrees and be careful to obey my regulations* (Ezekiel 36.26–27).

He had given her a new heart, a tender and responsive heart. And He had equipped her to embrace this messier middle, not in defeat but in victory.

She knew He was her refuge and safety.

Here's how Keri described it on her blog, "3 Stranded Cord":

*After I came to terms that nothing I did could save the pregnancy, I dove into Scripture. I had a choice, I could run to God and cling to the One who could hold me through it all, or I could run from Him and be utterly alone. As angry as I was with God and confused by Him, I knew enough that I needed Him, and I didn't go off my emotions but instead went with what I knew to be truth.*

*Will and I shared our real emotions and thoughts together as well, knowing that in our brokenness and honesty, healing begins. I turned to my Bible and found myself flipping between chapters in the book of Psalms. I was thankful I had underlined things through the years because I needed all the help I could get.*

*Over and over, sentence after sentence, as tears streamed down my face and I tried to find an answer for something I will never understand . . .* **I felt held.**

**"When I am afraid, I will trust in you."**

**"Cast your cares on the Lord and He will sustain you."**

**"For You are my fortress, my refuge in times of trouble."**

*God was speaking to me in a mighty way.*

**"Trust in Him at all times, O people; pour out your hearts to Him."** *And that's exactly what I did. I told Him I was exhausted on every level, I was in too deep of waters, and worn out from calling for help.*

*Then I came across this in Psalm 71:20:* **"Though you have made me see troubles, many and bitter, you will restore my life again; from the depths of the earth you will again bring me up."**

*I don't know how many more mis-carriages we will have, I don't know how many more children we will lose, I don't know a lot of things and that's okay, but what I do know at the end of the day, God is still God, and I'm still me and He sees a lot more than I will ever see!*[24]

You would think that one messier middle was enough to last a lifetime, but no, it continued with one difficult messier middle after another.

Months after Arabella's death, Keri experienced multiple devastating miscarriages before finally getting pregnant. And nine beautiful months after the last miscarriage, they were finally able to add another sweet baby girl to their family. Along with these challenges came a job loss for her husband, extreme difficulties with family members, and a multitude of daily living struggles.

I know Keri would be the first to tell you, she hates this messy middle living. It's gut-wrenchingly hard. She's broken. The heartache has been excruciating. She longs for heaven. But she has embraced this messy middleness better than anyone I know.

Keri is allowing God to shape and mold her in the pain. She has continued to keep her heart tender toward God as He shines His light on the ugly in her heart. And in so doing, she is living strong. She is living dangerously for God.

She is an example to us all of what it looks like to follow Jesus with our whole hearts and embrace the messy middle God calls each of us to WALK in.

## What About Us?

How will you keep your heart soft and pliable in the middle of the messiness of living in this fallen world?

---

24 3 Stranded Cord, August 28, 2016. www.3-strandedcord.blogspot.com.

## My prayer for you

*For your present troubles, _____, are small and won't last very long. Yet*
　　　　　　　　　　　　　*(insert name)*
*they produce for you a glory that vastly outweighs them and will last forever! So, you
don't look at the troubles you can see now; rather,* **fix your gaze***, _____,*
　　　　　　　　　　　　　　　　　　　　　　　　*(insert name)*
*on things that cannot be seen. For the things you see now will soon be gone, but the
things you cannot see will last forever.*

(Prayer based on 2 Corinthians 4.17–18)

## Will you dare to live dangerously and embrace the messy middle?

*Week 8*

# DARE TO LET GOD WRITE YOUR STORY

*Sometimes life takes us places we never expected to go, and in those places,*
*God writes a story we never thought would be ours.*

—RENEE SWOPE[25]

Everlasting father, I know in my head that the story You create is so much better than what I could ever write. But I am betrayed by my heart, somehow believing I can do a better job than You. How crazy is that? I'm sorry for my arrogance and I rest in Your forgiveness. Once again, I relinquish the pen and invite You to write Your story on the pages of my life. I am Yours forever. Amen.

---

25 Renee Swope, Facebook post, May 15, 2014.

# DAY 1
## AN ANCIENT STORY
# The Bleeding Woman

It was just one moment amongst thousands of moments in her sixty-plus years of living, but that one moment changed everything. She was long past this life-altering encounter, but it was forever etched in her memory.

She was not long for this world now. Her time was almost up, but she wasn't afraid. Death didn't scare her like it had. She had met her Savior and He had transformed her life. He had made her new in every way. Soon she would be with Him once again and this time it wouldn't be just one solitary moment but endless days in eternity with her Rescuer, her Savior, her Messiah. She could hardly wait. This imminent death was not the end of her journey, she knew it was just the beginning.

On this cool September morning, she had arisen early to watch the sunrise. All her bones seemed to creak within her as she made her way to her favorite chair by the window. She pulled a blanket off her mat and carefully placed it over her legs to keep her warm.

She loved this time of day. The way the sun broke through the darkness, casting its light on her. How it reflected off the sandstone-colored walls of her room and bathed her face in its warmth. She felt like a cat soaking up the morning sun. This time always took her back to the moment when the SON broke though the darkness of her soul and bathed her in the warmth of His love.

Even though it had been more than fifty years, not one day had passed without reminiscing about this one solitary moment in her life when everything changed. Even though she couldn't remember what she had for dinner last night, she knew every word He had said to her and every nuance of her encounter with Him.

She remembered the pain and desperation, like it was yesterday . . .

It was her "monthly flow" that wouldn't go away. Twelve long years of bleeding night and day. It was one doctor after another. Oh the shame and humility of it all. She could feel her body instinctively convulse as she remembered the horrible things they had done to her in their feeble attempts to heal her. She remembered the desperation in her heart. She just had to be cured even if it took every last coin she had. And it had. She was penniless and worse off than before she had gone to them.

She wasn't just broken physically, the wounds of her friends and family when they deserted her because of her "uncleanness" was almost more than she could bear. No one had wanted to be around her. They had quietly escorted her out of the village and left her with the other broken misfits. Ostracized and alone.

It started with whispered rumors passed around their little community. There was a Healer. He had made the blind see and the lame walk. He had cast out demons and healed lepers.

She was curiously skeptical. She had been through so much and she wasn't sure she had it in her to try one more thing. But the rumors persisted, and she could ignore them no longer.

She recalled how much she had wrestled in her heart about going to see Him. The fear had almost held her back. What would He do if she made Him unclean by touching her? She had only known condemnation from the Pharisees in her village. They had tossed her out of the village like a piece of garbage. Judge and jury declaring she must have done a terrible sin to have such a horrible disease.

Even now, remembering the excruciating pain of that moment brought fresh tears to her eyes. The shame and hurt had beaten her down so long she hardly knew who she was anymore. But hearing about this Rabbi, Jesus, had given her a glimmer of hope. He was different.

She finally mustered up enough strength and courage to go and see what all the commotion was about.

Standing at the edge of the crowd she listened to this man. She'd never heard any Rabbi speak with such authority. There was something so different about Him. She didn't know what it was then, but she knew now—it was love.

Captivated by the words He spoke, she had watched with surprise as Jairus, the leader from the local synagogue, interrupted Jesus. She could hear the desperation in his voice—she knew it all too well. The synagogue leader fell to his knees at the feet of Jesus and began to beg the Healer to go with him to heal his daughter. Awe filled her heart as she watched Jesus walk with Jairus to his home.

Her heart began to beat like a drum in her chest. She knew it was now or never. Her mind was racing. *If I can just touch the hem of His robe, I know I'll be healed. He won't have to stop where He's going, and no one will know.*

As she gazed out the window, lost in her thoughts of long ago, she chuckled at the memory. How foolish her well laid plans had been.

On that day so long ago, she had been a woman on a mission. Elbowing her way through the crowd, she was finally close enough to reach out and touch the Rabbi's robe. It happened so fast. One moment she was a woman who had bled for twelve interminable years and the next she was healed and whole. His healing power sent a shockwave surging through her body. She wondered if anyone around her saw what had just happened. How could they not, she wondered? This was earthshaking, life-altering.

As she glanced around she realized they were oblivious. Relieved that she wouldn't be the center of attention, she melted into the crowd. But she couldn't take her eyes off of Him. He had done what no one else could do!

With a start, she realized He knew.

He had stopped.

She watched as He turned to His disciples. "Someone touched me!"

They looked at Him like He was crazy.

Everything in her was screaming—*Run! Get out of here before He sees you.* But she could not will her legs to move.

"Of course, someone touched You. There are people all around us. Pressing in on every side." She could hear the sarcasm in their voices.

"No, someone touched me. I felt the healing power go out of me." He turned around and began searching for her. She could see His eyes roving over the crowd. She knew it was just a matter of time until He found her.

The old familiar fear threatened to choke the life out of her. What would He do to her?

She could see He wasn't giving up until He found her.

Shaking from head to toe, she stepped out of the crowd and into the empty circle surrounding Jesus. Falling to her knees at Jesus's feet, unable to look at His face, she spoke to His sandaled feet.

"Sir, I have had a terrible sickness. When I heard about you healing the blind, the lame, and the lepers, I knew you were like no man who had ever lived. I thought if I could just touch the hem of Your robe, I would be healed. And I was! If I have done something wrong . . ." Tears poured down her cheeks. Quietly she whispered, "Thank you, thank you."

Time stood still, the crowd disappeared.

It was just her and Jesus.

She saw His knees bend and His hand reach out toward her. She felt His gentle touch as He lifted her face to look into her eyes. She could see the love in His eyes. She could feel His forgiveness coursing through her soul, casting out the shame, healing her inside and out.

"Daughter, your faith has made you well. Go in peace. Your suffering is over."

Even now, she could feel those sweet words pouring over her dry thirsty soul, giving her life. He saw her. He knew her pain, her suffering. He understood the hardship she had been living under for so long. And wonder of wonders . . . He wasn't afraid to touch her. He had called her daughter!

As He was speaking to her, messengers from Jairus's home, arrived. "There is no need for Jesus to come because Jairus, your daughter has died."

*Oh no, I've kept Jesus from this man's daughter, and she has died because of me.* The fear was back with a vengeance. What would this crowd do to her? Would Jesus be angry?

But Jesus's words spoken to Jairus, were also a message to her. "Don't be afraid. Just have faith."

Faith in Jesus; it was what had healed her body, mind, and soul. Faith had replaced the all-consuming fear and allowed peace to reign.

She could see her life so clearly now all these years later. . . of course, hindsight always helps.

She had been so convinced she could do a better job than God at writing her story, that she had snatched the pen and attempted to write her own story. But her feeble attempts were just a jumbled mess of scribbles on the scroll of her life.

But that single, solitary encounter with Jesus had changed everything.

She had let go. *Why did it take me so long to see the truth?* She finally had surrendered to His authorship and allowed Him to write her story. And oh, what a beautiful story it was.

Soon she would see the Author of her story, once again and this time there would be no good-byes. She would spend forever in His presence. She couldn't wait because this wasn't the end of her story, it was just the beginning!

# Taking a Deeper Look

*In this section, it is your turn to take a deeper look at this story in God's Word and see for yourself the truth that lies within. These questions are intended to be a guide as you search for the treasure. If you don't know the answers to some of the questions, it's okay. Not knowing all the answers is not a bad thing. My hope is that it will cause you to think more deeply and explore Scripture in ways you might never have, if just given the answer.*

## MARK 5.21–36

*Jesus got into the boat again and went back to the other side of the lake, where a large crowd gathered around him on the shore. <sup>22</sup>Then a leader of the local synagogue, whose name was Jairus, arrived. When he saw Jesus, he fell at his feet, <sup>23</sup>pleading fervently with him. "My little daughter is dying," he said. "Please come and lay your hands on her; heal her so she can live."*

*<sup>24</sup>Jesus went with him, and all the people followed, crowding around him. <sup>25</sup>A woman in the crowd had suffered for twelve years with constant bleeding. <sup>26</sup>She had suffered a great deal from many doctors, and over the years she had spent everything she had to pay them, but she had gotten no better. In fact, she had gotten worse. <sup>27</sup>She had heard about Jesus, so she came up behind him through the crowd and touched his robe. <sup>28</sup>For she thought to herself, "If I can just touch his robe, I will be healed." <sup>29</sup>Immediately the bleeding stopped, and she could feel in her body that she had been healed of her terrible condition.*

## NOTES & OBSERVATIONS

Refer to page 8 for guidance on how to dig deeper into the story.

*Why was she so desperate? What do you learn about her from this passage?*

*What could Jesus have done instead when she touched His robe?*

³⁰Jesus realized at once that healing power had gone out from him, so he turned around in the crowd and asked, "Who touched my robe?"

³¹His disciples said to him, "Look at this crowd pressing around you. How can you ask, 'Who touched me?'"

³²But he kept on looking around to see who had done it. ³³Then the frightened woman, trembling at the realization of what had happened to her, came and fell to her knees in front of him and told him what she had done. ³⁴And he said to her, "Daughter, your faith has made you well. Go in peace. Your suffering is over."

³⁵While he was still speaking to her, messengers arrived from the home of Jairus, the leader of the synagogue. They told him, "Your daughter is dead. There's no use troubling the Teacher now."

³⁶But Jesus overheard them and said to Jairus, "Don't be afraid. Just have faith."

# REFLECTION

The desperation of this woman led her to seek out doctor after doctor, suffering much and at the end of the day, completely broke. She was worse off than when she had started. Lisa Terkeurst, in her book *Made to Crave,* says, "Desperation breeds defeat."[26] When we let our hearts run toward desperation, it will wear us down and cause us to compromise everything we once stood for.

1.    What has desperation driven you to do?

2.    How did Jesus respond to this bleeding woman?

3.    What does Jesus' response say to you?

**Note**: In the eyes of the community, this woman had two things against her; she was a woman, and she had a disease.

---

26 Lisa Teurkerst, *Made to Crave Devotional* (Grand Rapids: Zondervan, 2011), 149.

4. What does Jesus's response to this woman say to the crowd?

5. What does His response say to her?

# DAY 2
# GOD'S BIGGER STORY

## Who will write your story?

Everyone has a story. The real question is—Who will write it? You or God?

The author of a book has the power with his or her pen to write a beautiful or tragic story. They are the ones with all the power. The characters must be who the writer dictates them to be and do what the writer directs them to do. It is laughable to think that a character in a story would demand she be queen of the kingdom rather than a peasant enslaved in the castle.

And God is the original Author of every story walking around on this planet. He is the One who made us. We are His design.

Look at what my friend Holly, shares regarding what scientists have discovered about our DNA.

*Each sperm and egg hold exactly half of the DNA needed to form a new person. Every sperm and egg is unique from the others containing threads of genetic information from the mother and father and their ancestors.*

*After the sperm enters the egg, the tightly wound threads of DNA within the egg and the sperm unravel themselves and then "weave" themselves together within the new cell to create a whole new genetic code and unique human being.*

David penned in Psalm 139.13, *"You made all the delicate, inner parts of my body and **knit** me together in my mother's womb."*

This is not just poetic language, it is truth. God does knit us together, exactly like He says! He knows our every thread of DNA. He wove us together in our mother's womb using the genetic materials that He created. He designed the process so that you would be uniquely you. His story![27]

---

27  PBS "Life's Greatest Miracle" documentary, 2001

# Writing Our Own Story

Sadly, humanity doesn't like the story God is writing. We shake our fists and demand things be written our way.

It started with Adam and Eve and continues with us. Each one of us has wrestled the pen from God's grasp and chosen to become the author of our own destiny (Isaiah 53.6).

Sin has decimated our world. Humanity's ascribed stories are atrocious. But Christ came to offer us a better way. He came so we might return the pen to its original author and allow Him to write our beautiful story.

When we invite Christ into our lives, we are essentially handing Him back the pen and surrendering our story to His authorship. But so often, even though we have returned the pen to its rightful owner, our propensity is to take it back and author our own stories, convinced we can do a as good a job as God, maybe even better. We tell ourselves that when we are the author with sole authority orchestrating predictable outcomes, it is safer. Less risky.

And that is exactly what Satan wants us to believe.

If he can get us to believe we can write a better story than this unpredictable God, then we are no threat to Satan or his kingdom of darkness.

He doesn't have to be concerned about us with our live-safe mentality and predictable lives. Choosing comfort over radical obedience. Allowing fear to paralyze us and safety to minimize us. The father of lies has us right where he wants us to be.

But really isn't it just easier to write our own story? Then we can have what we want and do what we want. We won't have an interfering God who allows the unpredictable in our lives.

At least that's what we tell ourselves to justify yanking the pen from His hand.

But ALWAYS there is chaos and dissonance with our feeble attempts to write our own story.

# A KitchenAid Mixer

There was a period of time (unfortunately, this wasn't the only time) where I was disillusioned with the narrative God was writing, so I decided to take things into my own hands and write the story I wanted.

It took a Kitchen Aid mixer to reveal the ugly buried deep inside.

Soon after my husband and I were married, I developed a burning desire to have a Kitchen Aid mixer. I loved making homemade bread and cinnamon rolls but hated kneading the dough and just knew that a Kitchen Aid mixer was the answer to all my problems!

Unfortunately, my husband didn't share this same conviction. (At least I didn't think he did and this mixer was pretty expensive for our one-salary income.) So as the years went by with no mixer in sight my burning desire became a blazing inferno. I just had to get a Kitchen Aid mixer.

During this time, a young couple moved in next door. Our houses were extremely close. I could look through my kitchen window right into their dining room and on into their kitchen.

This couple seemed to have everything going for them. I stared with envy as they put marble countertops in their kitchen and redecorated every room in their house.

The final straw came one day when I was happily cooking away in my kitchen and gazed into their dining room and on into their kitchen.

*What is that sitting on her kitchen counter? Is it a—? No! It can't be! For cryin' out loud, it's a Kitchen Aid mixer!*

*Why does she have that and not me? She never cooks. Here I am slaving and sacrificing to follow You, Jesus, and what have You given me? Nothing. She's not even a follower, yet she gets everything she wants! God this just isn't fair. I don't like this story You're writing for me. I want a new one, in fact I'll just take hers.*

God took a scalpel to my heart that day when He asked, "Kristi, what are you really believing about Me? What's buried deep in your heart?"

It pains me to put this to print. My jealous heart had tricked me into believing that God was not good. He didn't really love me because if He really loved me, if He was really good, then He would give me what I wanted.

I was a child who didn't like the beautiful story Jesus was writing for me. I grabbed the pen and scribbled all over His work, convinced my scribbles were better than His.

# We Aren't the Main Character in the Story

Ephesians 2.10 says, *"For we are God's masterpiece."* We are His work of art. His story.

Just as a work of art gives glory to the artist or a beautifully crafted story gives homage to the author, so we, as **God's stories,** should give glory to our Author.

Paul tells us in Ephesians, *"But God is so rich in mercy, and he loved us so much, that even though we were dead because of our sins, he gave us life when He raised Christ from the dead."* And because of what Christ has done for us, **"God can point to us in all** *future ages as examples of the incredible wealth of his grace and kindness toward us"* (Ephesians 2.4–5, 7).

Do you see it? We are His bragging rights. He's like a grandparent who readily whips out pictures when asked about their grandkids. When talking with the angels, He points to us and says, "That's My daughter. She's My special work of art. Look at what I have done in her. Isn't she beautiful?" We are living testimonies proclaiming His glory, not our own.

While recently reading my good friend Shannon Popkin's book, *Comparison Girl,* I was reminded that even though God is writing my story, I'm not the main character in it—He is! This story is not about me—it's about Him.

Shannon writes, "The whole world tells the story about our Creator. Each chapter of earth's history chronicles a new detailed account of God. Yes, you and I are tucked into tiny paragraphs. Our lives are important and seen. But every line of the story showcases His glory, not ours."[28]

When I snatch the pen from God and attempt to write my own story, I diminish His glory and point people to me, not Him. I showcase my glory, not His.

## Knowing Our Ending

What kind of reader are you? Are you a reader of endings first?

Monica Edinger in her blog, *Educating Alice,* confesses that she is a reader of endings first. She shares that when reading a series of books where she has gotten to know and care about the characters that she needs to read the ending. Look at her reasoning, "I knew as I began reading that I needed that worry set at rest so I could get into the book to enjoy the adventure, to find out how they made it safely to the end." She also gives another reason why she might read the ending first: "I might find it slow going and rather than immediately quitting, I might check further along to see if something there made it worth continuing."[29]

Friends, **we know the ending of our story**. One day all the pain and sorrow of this world will vanish, and we will see in brilliant colors the whole of our story. All the missing pieces will fall into place. We will

---

28 Shannon Popkin, *Comparison Girl* (Grand Rapids: Kregel, 2020), 53.
29 Educating Alice, Monica Edinger, January 30, 2008 post, **The Right to Read the End First | educating alice (wordpress.com).**

fall at Jesus's feet and worship Him as we see His finished masterpiece in us.

For now, let us trust the Author of our story and enjoy the journey He has written for us because after all, **we know our ending**.

In case you're letting fear keep you from trusting, let me remind you. This Author of your story left the glories and beauty of heaven to dwell in the slums we call earth. He died a horrible death on a cross and was raised again so that you might know your ending.

You see, when we KNOW the author of our story, we will trust the masterpiece He is creating, even if we can't see it.

*Why do you question the beautiful narrative He is writing for you?*

*What causes you to doubt His goodness?*

*What more could He do to prove His passionate love for you?*

## *Enjoying the Adventure*

In college, I took a camping class for a semester and one of the requirements for the class was a weekend backpacking trip in Northern Michigan.

Before we began our infamous weekend, our guide had a few things to share with us. He told us we would be cooking our own meals, rafting down a river, and climbing a hundred-foot tree to zip line across the river. I can remember so clearly him finishing up his little chat by saying, "Everyone is required to go across the zip line. There are no ifs,

ands, or buts about it, and if you take too long, I will push you off the branch!" Yikes.

I sat on the bank of the river and watched as intrepid team members slowly climbed up the tree and zipped across the river. Our guide's nine-year-old son took his turn before me. He made it about half-way up before he melted down. Sobbing loudly, arms wrapped tightly around the tree, he refused to budge.

I was intrigued as I watched this rough, tough, push-you-off-the-branch guide climb the tree to his son. I thought for sure he was going to make him climb the rest of the way up and zip line across. After all, he did say everybody.

But the man climbing up the tree to rescue his son, wasn't the rough, tough guide we'd been introduced to; he was a father concerned for his child.

I watched as he talked with his son for quite a while before helping him climb down step by slow step. Then he proceeded to put his son on his shoulders and step into the icy waters to cross the river. (It was springtime in Michigan and the river was a rushing torrent of melted snow.) We held our breath as he slipped on the rocks and worked against the current to carry his son across.

Forever stamped on my memory is the sight of this young boy on his daddy's shoul-ders. All the fear he had while climbing the tree was gone. He was smiling and laughing and waving at us as his daddy carried him safely across the river. Completely oblivious to the peril of the river, he was enjoying the journey.

Think for a second about this beautiful picture of a father's love for his son and the son's unwavering trust in his father. Could this be the way *God* wants us to live? Could this be how He wants us to respond when the river is rushing and the water is scary. Even when our situations seem impossible and the future is daunting, does God want us to trust Him like this boy trusted his father? Is God inviting us to climb up on His shoulders and not just simply hold on for dear life but enjoy the ride?

# Dangerous Living

Shadrach, Meschach, and Abednego were three young, enslaved Jewish boys who knew their ending and it gave them the boldness and courage to defy a king.

King Nebuchadnezzar had ordered everyone in the kingdom to bow down and worship his statue. Anyone who didn't comply would be thrown into the fiery furnace, but these three dared to defy the king and refused to bow down.

The king was furious when he found out they had not bowed down. He had them brought before him to give them one last chance to obey. The King said angrily, *"If you don't obey we will throw you into the blazing furnace and then what god will be able to rescue you from my power?"*

Their simple reply speaks volumes as to what they believed and how they were choosing to live. *"O Nebuchadnezzar,* **we do** *not need to defend ourselves before you. If we are thrown into the blazing furnace, **the God whom we serve is able to save us**. He will rescue us from your power, Your Majesty. **But even if he doesn't,** we want to make it clear to you, Your Majesty, that we will never serve your gods or worship the gold statue you have set up"* (Daniel 3.16–18).

We, too, know our ending! We are safe and secure in the Master's plan. Will we be brave and embrace the story God is writing for us? Will we say, as Shadrach, Meschach, and Abednego said, "I know You can save me from this hardship and struggle but even if You don't, I still choose You"? This, my friends, is Dangerous Living.

**God wants to write your story, but He will never wrestle the pen from your grasp.**

Our natural tendency is to want to create our own narrative. It's scary to let someone else be in control. But remember what this God was willing to do for you. Will He not do what is best?

God wants to write a story so much bigger and better than you could ever dream possible. *"No eye has seen, no ear hs heard, no mind has imagined what God has prepared for those who love Him"* (1 Corinthians 2.9).

However, this doesn't mean the story He is writing for you will not be fraught with difficulty, struggles, and hardship. In fact, Jesus told us it would be anything but comfortable: *"The gateway to life is very narrow and the road is difficult, and only a few ever find it"* (Matthew 7.14).

**This difficult way is the road to life**, but the sure hope we have is this—**we do not walk alone**. *"You are a chosen people. You are royal priests, a holy nation, God's very own possession. As a result, you can show others the goodness of God, for He called you out of the darkness into his wonderful light"* (1 Peter 2.9).

He loves us with an everlasting love. His demonstration of love is the greatest expression of love known to man. What more could He do to prove He is for us?

My friend, will you relinquish the pen, and embrace the adventure God wants to write for you?

# DAY 3
# DIG DEEPER INTO THE STORY

## ROMANS 11.33–12.2

*Oh, how great are God's riches and wisdom and knowledge! How impossible it is for us to understand His decisions and His ways!*

*[34] For who can know the LORD's thoughts? Who knows enough to give Him advice? [35] And who has given Him so much that He needs to pay it back? [36] For everything comes from Him and exists by His power and is intended for His glory. All glory to Him forever! Amen.*

*12.[1] And so, dear brothers and sisters, I plead with you to give your bodies to God because of all He has done for you. Let them be a living and holy sacrifice—the kind He will find acceptable. This is truly the way to worship Him. [2] Don't copy the behavior and customs of this world, but let God transform you into a new person by changing the way you think. Then you will learn to know God's will for you, which is good and pleasing and perfect.*

## NOTES & OBSERVATIONS

Refer to page 8 for guidance on how to dig deeper into the story.

*What do we learn about God in Romans 11?*

*Why is it essential for the readers of Romans to be reminded of these aspects of God's character? (Note: Many of the Romans believers this was written to were under severe persecution for their faith.)*

1.  What are we to do as a result of knowing God and His character (Romans 12.1)?

    Why?

2.  What is a living and holy sacrifice? (Take each word, look up the meaning in a dictionary and ponder their meaning.)

    Living:

    Holy:

    Sacrifice:

3.  How does Paul define worship?

4.  What are we not to do (v. 2)?

    What are we to do?

5.  Why is it our "thinking" that God transforms and not our "behavior"?

6.  Are you willing to surrender the pen to the Master who wants to transform *your story* into His beautiful masterpiece?

    If not, what's holding you back?

# DAY 4
# PAUSE AND REFLECT ON THE STORY

*Lord, you are mine! I promise to obey your words! With all my heart I want your blessings.*
*Be merciful as you promised. I pondered the direction of my life, and I turned to follow your laws.*
—PSALM 119.57–59

What has God been speaking to you regarding what you have just read and studied in Chapter 8?

What challenged you?

What encouraged you?

# Spiritual Appraisal

When we aren't surrendering our life to God, we are not worshipping Him. It is a simple as that. Attending church and singing praises to God with His people convince us that we are worshipping, but often our lives remain a glaring contradiction. Remember, God is looking for true worshippers who will worship Him **in spirit and in truth**.

Are you allowing God to write your story in every area of your life?

Think of your life as a house with many rooms. Are you willing to let God invade every room, corner, nook and cranny, closet, basement and dungeon of your life? Are there rooms you're preventing Him from entering?

*Search me, O God, and know my heart; test me and know my anxious thoughts. Point out anything in me that offends you, and lead me along the path of everlasting life.*

—Psalm 139.23–24

What are you hiding from God? Spend some quiet time with God, walking through the rooms of your life—open cupboards, look under beds, walk down into the dungeon, and allow Him to see the sin lurking in your heart. It might look something like this, "Lord is there anything in this room—my relationship room—that is holding me back and not allowing me to walk in victory? Where I'm attempt-

Journal your thoughts.

ing to write my own story instead of surrendering to You?"

**Relationship Room:** Is there anything broken in my relationship with— God, spouse, children, friends, family members, etc.

**Emotions Room:** Am I letting feelings control my decisions—depression, discouragement, pride, worry, etc.

**Physical Room:** Am I taking care of my body? Am I overly consumed with my body image? Am I allowing food to be my god - by purging, anorexia or just constantly thinking about it? Is time management a problem? etc.

**Thought-life Room:** Am I dissatisfied with how God made me? What lies am I believing? I have allowed doubt, discouragement, bitterness, etc. to become my focus? Am I harboring unforgiveness for someone? etc.

**Spiritual Room:** Am I distant, stagnant, fear-controlled, lost, wavering, hard-hearted, etc.?

**Dungeon:** Are there things I am trying desperately to hide from God and others—the hurt I have done to myself or others have done to me, sins from my past that seem unforgiveable, and the refusal to give forgive yourself?

Once those areas are revealed, confess them. Acknowledge how your actions and attitudes have broken your relationship with God and claim the forgiveness He's already extended to you. Then move on.

The more voice you can give voice to the angst and sin in your heart, the more the ugly is brought into the Light. This then gives space for you and God to deal with it together. Don't be afraid to sit in the uncomfortable—this is where God wants to do His great work in you.

Are there areas where you have experienced growth and victory? Give praise to God for His amazing work in your life.

# Read Outloud

*Take a minute to picture Jesus sitting next to you. He has gently turned your face to His because He wants you to listen to what He has to say. Don't just brush past this, let its truth sink into your soul.*

I see you . . .

I know you . . .

I love you . . .

You are the apple of my eye (Psalm 17.8).

I remember the day you were a blotch of nothing waiting to be a something. A lifeless form awaiting the Hand of the Designer. I took my time as I molded each part of you (Psalm 139.13). Your hands and heart, your legs and ears, your mind and personality, your temperament. I put a part of Me in you (Genesis 1.27).

I know every hair on your head (Matthew 10.30). I know when you sit and when you stand. I know your own thoughts even before you think them (Psalm 139.4). You are precious to me. My thoughts of you are as endless as the sand on the seashore (Psalm 139.17–18). You are my child, my creation, my design. You are my bright, shining star, and my love for you is everlasting (Philippians 2.15).

How I long for you to know Me (Jeremiah 9.24).

I see how you turn away from Me to other things. I watch you seek love in loveless, fickle beings instead of me. I see you searching the garbage dump for hidden treasures, trading beauty for filth (1 Samuel 2.8). My heart breaks each time I see you wander from one empty moment to another.

Do you know that from the beginning of time I knew you would turn away from me? But that did not stop Me from devising the most unbelievable and shocking plan the heavens have ever seen. No one was more astounded than the angels at My grand design; the God of the Universe laying down His life for the ones He created. And I did it without reservation—for you!

Why? Because I'm crazy about you (Zephaniah 3.17). I'm smitten with you. I want you as My own. This love I have for you has no bounds and knows no limits. The depth and breadth and height of My love is beyond your comprehension. The only other love you have ever experienced has been limited, minute, and insignificant, but My love transcends all other love (Ephesians 3.18–19).

But it is your choice to accept or deny.

You may know about this extravagant gift of love. You may even have accepted my gift. But I feel you holding back. Afraid. Apprehensive. Unsure. What will this God ask of me, you wonder? What will He require?

I see you comparing, judging, holding Me up to the light of others who have loved you and let you down, who have broken their promises and abandoned you.

Remember . . . I love you with an *everlasting love.*

You are My most treasured possession (James 1.18).

I will not let you go, abandon you, or break My promises to you; that's not who I AM (Daniel 9.4).

I long for you to WANT Me. KNOW Me (Jeremiah 9.23–24).

COME to Me (Matthew 11.28–29).

SURRENDER your very being to Me, for in the surrendering you will find life and in the knowing you will discover freedom (John 8.36).

My precious daughter, you have written your own story long enough and where has it left you? Broken, confused, and disillusioned. Will you surrender the pen to Me? Will you let Me write the beautiful story I have planned for you?

I'm waiting.

# DAY 5
# DARE TO LIVE THE STORY
## *Kristi*

MY HEART WAS POUNDING! *WHATEVER possessed me to even think this was a good idea?* Trembling from head to toe, I glanced over the side of our tiny platform to the rushing Great Zambizi river three hundred feet below. *Clearly, not the smartest thing I've ever done. This is insane!*

As we stood on the platform getting harnessed in with all the straps and buckles by a nice African man, my friend asked him, "Have you ever done this?"

There was a loud explosion of air from his mouth as he replied, "No!"

*Well, now, that was encouraging.*

Months before, my friend and I had glibly agreed to do this crazy jump over the Great Zambezi river in Zimbabwe. We were excited that we could do a tandem jump, never really considering the insanity of it all—a two-hundred-fifty-foot free-fall jump in a foreign country, over crocodile infested waters. It had all seemed so easy and exciting from the comfort of our own homes, thousands of miles away. Seriously, what were we thinking!

As my friend and I stood there shaking that day, on our tiny platform high above the crocodile infested waters, the nice young man, who had never-ever jumped, calmly told us to move closer to the edge. *Are you nuts?* I wanted to yell at him. Everything in me was shouting to do just the opposite. He began the countdown.

"**3-2-1 JUMP!**"

Amazingly, we did.

As soon as we jumped, my fear was gone! Astonishingly, euphoric even! It felt like we were falling in slow motion. I can still see my friend's ponytail, as if it were being pulled by a cord straight above her head.

When we finished, we looked at each other and yelled, "Let's do it again!"

Little did I know it then, but just a few short months later, God would ask me to take an even bigger leap of faith.

For most of my life I have wanted to be a missionary in a foreign field. I believe God calls all of us to be missionaries—sharing our faith with those around us—but some He calls to distant lands, and I wanted to be one of those. My parents had been missionaries in Alaska, and my sole desire while growing up was to become a missionary just like them.

I went off to Bible school with my heart set on the mission field. But it was at a small mission's retreat that God changed the course of my life.

The speaker had been a missionary in China for ten years before the Communist party came into power. When they took over China, he and his wife had to drop everything and literally run for their lives. He openly shared his struggle with God as he wrestled with feelings of abandonment and disillusionment. He testified how good God had been as he sat with the Lord and shared his feelings. Then he followed that by telling of the beautiful restoration God brought as he walked with God through his grief and loss.

As I listened to him share, the thought crossed my mind . . . *Am I pursuing missions because it is what God wants me to do or because I want to do it?* That shook me.

Late that night, I sat out on a dock and dipped my feet in the water. As I reflected on this life-altering thought I'd had while listening to this missionary, I sensed God asking, "Kristi, will you follow Me even if I never call you to go overseas?"

I know many of you have the opposite struggle: "Please don't send me overseas, God." But for me missions in a foreign field had been my great desire, the thing I had been working so hard all my life to achieve. Now God was asking me to surrender this dream to Him.

I believe God requests complete surrender from every person who sincerely says, "I want to follow You, Jesus." And that whole-hearted surrender always requires relinquishing the thing we hold most dear.

We see this with the rich young ruler in Matthew 19.16–22. The young man came to Jesus and said, "I've kept all the commandments, what else do I need to do to have eternal life?"

Jesus told him, "Sell all your possessions and give to the poor and then come follow Me."

What Jesus was saying to this man was, "Let go of what you hold most dear and come follow Me." And the man couldn't do it.

Another time, Jesus told the crowd following Him, *"If you want to be my disciple, you must, by comparison, hate everyone else— your father and mother, wife and children, brothers and sisters—yes, even your own life. Otherwise, you cannot be my disciple. And if you do not carry your own cross and follow me, you cannot be my disciple"* (Luke 14.26–27).

If you want to follow, truly follow Jesus, He will always ask you to surrender whatever it is you hold most dear.

Will you follow me if I never give you children?

Will you follow me if you never get married?

Will you follow me if you will always struggle financially?

Will you follow me if I ask you to leave the job you love?

Will you follow me if . . . ?

Why does He do this? Why does He ask us to let go of the thing we hold most dear?

Because He knows, *"wherever your treasure is, there the desires of your heart will be as well"* (Matthew 6.21).

What we love holds our heart.

The love that held my heart was my dream not God's. I had essentially yanked the pen from His hand and attempted to write my own story. I was following my way not Jesus'.

In this sacred moment out on the dock, just as He did with the rich young ruler, Jesus brought into the light the real treasure of my heart.

"Will you follow me, Kristi, if I never let you go overseas?"

Jesus is good at asking poignant questions. Questions that go straight to the heart. Peeling away all the layers in one simple question.

Jesus often asked these layer-peeling questions of His disciples.

One day Jesus spoke some really hard-to-understand, tough-stuff to the crowd of people following Him. Many shook their heads and walked away. Jesus turned to the twelve and asked a layer-peeling question: "Will you leave me too?"

Even though they too did not understand what Jesus was saying, they **knew** the man who was saying these difficult things. I love Peter's response. In John 6.68–69, Peter essentially says, "Where would we go? You have the words of Eternal Life. You are the Holy One of God" (John 6.68–69).

Like the disciples, this was God's layer-peeling question for me, and like Peter,

I said, "Where would I go? You have the words of eternal life. You are the Holy One of God. Yes Lord, I will follow You wherever you lead me."

It was my watershed moment as I relinquished my pen and returned it to its rightful owner.

Just months later, I started dating a man who would become my husband. God had called him to be a missionary in the secular work world, but not overseas. God's refining moment allowed me to embrace this calling and walk alongside him.

We had four crazy, turn-your-hair-gray boys, and I was focused on being their mom. As I was raising them, God began to cultivate His desire in me to go to the mission field. I saw my neighborhood of moms as my mission field and began to pour into their lives. But still the draw to do missions overseas grew stronger and stronger with each passing year.

With not one opportunity for even a short-term mission's trip, I could feel the anger rising up in me. *Why would You put this desire in me and never let me go?* It just didn't make sense. I was disillusioned with God and jealous with everyone else who had opportunities to go. I hated the ugly place I was in and pleaded with God to take it away.

But God refused to answer my request, and the desire to minister overseas continued. I received no explanation, just a quiet call to trust Him and be faithful where He had me. I wish I could say I did that and did it well, but sadly I can't. It was many years of wrestling with God and buckets of tears before I finally embraced where He had placed me.

During this time, I served for more than eight years as the women's ministry director at my church. My focus was discipling, training, mentoring, and challenging women to live dangerously for God. I had been on staff for almost seven years when I saw this God-given dream finally become a reality. I was invited to go on my very first missions' trip to the Dominican Republic.

On that trip, I soaked up every precious moment and every sweet encounter with women who were so different from me and yet the same in so many ways. I returned the following year to lead a team of women from our church.

On our flight home, my boss turned to me and said, "I had a dream about you last night."

"You did?"

"Yeah, and I don't even want to tell you. Seriously, it makes me want to throw up."

I hesitantly asked her to tell me what it was.

"I dreamed you went into missions."

I burst into tears right there on our airplane, not caring who saw.

"I would do that tomorrow, if I could!" I replied through my tears.

"Kristi, you do your job really well, but you were different here. It's so clear this is what you were made for."

"I would do this tomorrow, but I don't know what I can do."

"I don't know either," she replied, "but let's pray about it."

And so we did.

In January of 2016, just six months after this conversation, I chose "dare" as my focus word for the year. I began to pray every day, "God, I dare to BE who you want me to be. I dare to SAY what you want me to say. I dare to DO what you want me to do. I dare to GO wherever you call me to go." As I prayed this prayer, I felt God put within me a confidence that if I took Him up on every dare He put before me, my life was going to look completely different come January 2017. I didn't know exactly how, but I knew without a shadow of a doubt I would never be the same again.

The most astonishing thing about choosing "dare" as my word of the year was that this fearful girl was no longer afraid. God had replaced my fear with an unwavering trust in Him.

My first dare came by way of Facebook messenger. A friend in California, whom I had gone to school with, asked me if I wanted to go with him and a few others to train women in discipleship in India. We had not seen each other in more than thirty years.

I was stunned and immediately responded yes!

As I continued to pray my dare prayer, God threw down more dares and I responded to each one with a resounding yes. God continued to open wide the doors, and I followed one simple step at a time. By January of 2017, I had resigned my position as women's ministry director at my church and stepped into the world of missions work overseas. What I had been doing for years in my church, training and discipling women, God would use all those skills in creating a global ministry to women.

This would not be just a short term trip but a long term commitment to serve the women of the world. It would mean working online throughout the year and visiting periodically, building relationships with women and men so that I might understand better how to come alongside them in their ministries and serve them.

I was amazed by God's timing and humbled by His forethought. I could see so clearly how He had been preparing me all along for this moment. *Why did I question? Why did I doubt?*

It was terrifying to leave my well-paid, secure position where I was influencing women and God was blessing in powerful ways. The edge of the platform anxiety felt like deja vu.

I had done this before . . .

Suddenly, I was back on the tiny platform in Zimbabwe staring down at the crocodile infested waters, but instead of an African man counting down, it was God.

But this time was different. The "countdowner" wasn't standing on the sidelines, He had taken my hand and walked with me to the edge of the cliff.

"Kristi, I've got this. Do you trust me?"

**"3-2-1 Jump!"**

And *we* did.

## What About You?

What self-made dream are you willing to let go of to follow God with your whole heart?

What God-given dream is being held captive out of reasonableness in your life? Why?

Are you willing to pray a dangerous prayer?

*God I dare to be whoever You want me to be.*
*I dare to say whatever You want me to say.*
*I dare to do whatever You want me to do.*
*And I dare to go wherever You want me to go.*

# A Prayer Over You

Lord, you alone are _____ inheritance, her cup of
<br>
*(insert your name)*
<br>
blessing.

You guard all that is hers. The land you have given her is a pleasant land. What a wonderful inheritance!

_____ will bless the Lord who guides her; even at night
<br>
*(insert your name)*
<br>
her heart instructs her.

She knows the Lord is always with her. She will not be shaken, for You are right beside her. No wonder her heart is glad, and she rejoices. _____
<br>
*(insert your name)*
<br>
body rests in safety. For You will not leave her soul among the dead or allow your holy one to rot in the grave. You will show her the way of life, granting her the joy of Your presence and the pleasures of living with You forever.

(Prayer based on Psalm 16.5–11)

Will you dare to live dangerously and let God write your story?

# Afterword

*"Courage is shaking in your boots and saddling up anyway!"*

—JOHN WAYNE

FRIENDS, WE WILL ALWAYS HAVE FEAR. BUT LET ME REMIND YOU THAT 2 TIMOTHY 1.7 SAYS THAT God HAS NOT GIVEN US a spirit of fear, but He has given us His Holy Spirit—His Spirit of love, power, and self-discipline. He is our Comforter. He fills us with the courage to rise up and speak His truth, and be the princess warriors our Heavenly Father is calling each one of us to be.

This warriorship is not just for pastors and leaders in the church. This is a commission given to each one of us. Look at what Paul says in 2 Corinthians 2.14–16: "*But thank God! He has made us his captives and continues to lead us along in Christ's triumphal procession.* **Now he uses US to spread the knowledge of Christ everywhere,** *like a sweet perfume.* **Our lives are a Christ-like fragrance rising up to God.** *But this fragrance is perceived differently by those who are being saved and by those who are perishing. To those who are perishing, we are a dreadful smell of death and doom. But to those who are being saved, we are a life-giving perfume. And who is adequate for such a task as this?*"

This is again the upside-down Kingdom of Jesus where captives become warriors spreading the knowledge of Christ everywhere. As captives we have surrendered to our victor, Jesus—we have laid down our passions and desires and He has replaced them with His. And now He calls us to live as His warriors spreading the truth everywhere.

Living dangerously for God doesn't necessarily mean we will have to sell everything and move to the jungles of Papua New Guinea, but it does mean we **must** loosen our grip on all that we hold dear and choose to follow, whether we're in a blue recliner giving praise to the One who has made us His captives, or on our knees doing battle with the enemy in our bedroom. Whether we are in a messy middle, caring for a hard to love parent, or living in the heart of Africa. The call is the same for every follower.

*"If anyone wants to follow in my footsteps, he must give up all right to himself, take up his cross and follow me" (Matthew 16.24* PHILLIPS*).*

The message of Jesus has always been polarizing: **"I am the Way, the Truth and the Life, no one comes to the Father except through Me"** (John 14.6). Paul says that to some this message is a life-giving perfume, but to others it is the smell of death. This is the difficult road of following Christ. Some will respond and others will turn their backs on us and walk away. Some will welcome us with open arms and others will spit on us and beat us.

In our comfy American life, few of us have ever faced serious persecution. We have settled into our cozy lifestyles and allowed the messages of the world to color our view and dictate our behavior. We have settled for mediocrity rather than radical obedience. But this is not the way of Jesus, this is not the message Jesus came to bring.

He is . . .

THE WAY

THE TRUTH,

and THE LIFE.

Will you leave your life of mediocrity behind and dare to live dangerously for God?

*This is what the Lord says:*

> *"Stand at the crossroads and look;*
> *ask for the ancient paths,*
> *ask where the good way is, and walk in it,*
> *and you will find rest for your souls."*

—Jeremiah 6.16 NIV

We are at the crossroads. You are at a crossroad.

One is the difficult road that leads to life. The other is the easy, comfortable road, but never forget, the easy path leads to death (Matthew 7.13–14)!

Friend, there is no middle ground. Deciding not to choose is still a choice. Which one will you choose?

Jesus said, *"The thief's purpose is to steal, kill and destroy. But I have come that they might have life and have it to the full"* (John 10.10, NIV).

Jesus cautions us to "count the cost" before we commit to following Him. His way is the road less traveled. It is the path of dangerous living, but this is where the adventure begins, and where TRUE LIFE is found. Will you choose HIS WAY every day? I dare you!

# Acknowledgments

Harold, thank you for loving me unconditionally and sacrificing so much to see my dreams come true. You continue to challenge me to dare to live dangerously and follow Jesus with my whole heart. I'm so deeply grateful to God for giving you to me.

To my amazing adult children: Wes, Sean, Lincoln, Logan and Yohan. You taught me so much about myself and what it means to trust Jesus fully. My deepest desire for you is that you will love Jesus with your whole heart, dare to live dangerously for God and lead your families to do the same.

Karen and Karla, I'm so grateful to God for the gift He gave me in you. You are not only my sisters but my dearest friends (and not many can say that about family). You've been there to listen and walk with me through the hard times. And now that our sweet mama is gone, the treasure of you has become even more precious. Thank you for stepping in and filling the role of our dear mama.

Shannon Popkin, truly this book would not have been written if it weren't for your belief in me. Your constant encouragement to not listen to the enemy but write the message God gave me, was exactly what I needed. Our meeting at Grand Traverse Pie Company was a game changer for me. Thank you, friend, for believing in me, when I didn't believe in myself.

Sarah Flick, you are a kindred spirit. I cherish our times together and thank God for a friend like you who always challenges and pushes me to be more.

Lisa Finkel, I never dreamed that first year in our small group would lead to such a deep, heart-to-heart relationship with you. You truly are my iron-sharpening-iron friend. Thank you for the sacrifices you have made to stand with me in serving women around the world.

Erjona, Rhodess, Ibu Lydia, Noku, Josephine, Winnie, you are my treasured international friends who continue to show me what it looks like to follow Jesus with my whole heart. Thank you for daring to live dangerously and showing me the way. My life is so much richer and fuller for having each of you in it.

Chris Kanai, Heather Rangel, Kim Seymour, Keri Ellis, Tricia Maynard, Merrily Lee, Joy Rohrer, Caurey Byers, Carolyn Frank, Victoria Paffile, Arva VandenPloeg, thank you friends for wading through the unedited version of this book. You are true friends.

Sarah DeMey, this book is so much better because of you. Thank you for investing yourself in the editing of this book.

Precious Jesus, thank you for daring to live dangerously, first. Thank you for choosing to leave the beauty of heaven to rescue me. I owe you everything. May my life and this book bear witness to Your great love. And may each woman who reads this book dare to follow in Your footsteps and live dangerously for You!

Made in the USA
Middletown, DE
15 August 2023

36246338R00133